+

2017/2018

SUMMERWORKS

- 2023 July - Canadian audio 1

2023 Feb-May - URBANDOG Servies

SUMMERWORKS

GREAT PLAYS from the INDIE THEATRE FESTIVAL

edited by

MICHAEL RUBENFELD

PLAYWRIGHTS CANADA PRESS
TORONTO • CANADA

PLAYWRIGHTS CANADA PRESS
The Canadian Drama Publisher
215 Spadina Ave., Suite 230, Toronto, Ontario Canada M5T 2C7
phone 416.703.0013 fax 416.408.3402
orders@playwrightscanada.com • www.playwrightscanada.com

The publisher acknowledges the support of the Canadian taxpayers through the Government of Canada Book Publishing Industry Development Program, the Canada Council for the Arts, the Ontario Arts Council, and the Ontario Media Development Corporation.

Canada

Canada Council for the Arts / Conseil des Arts du Canada

ONTARIO ARTS COUNCIL / CONSEIL DES ARTS DE L'ONTARIO

Ontario
Ontario Media Development Corporation

Cover design by Leah Renihan
Type design by Blake Sproule

LIBRARY AND ARCHIVES CANADA CATALOGUING IN PUBLICATION

Summerworks : great plays from the Indie Theatre Festival / Michael Rubenfeld, ed.

ISBN 978-0-88754-871-0

1. Canadian drama (English)--21st century. I. Rubenfeld, Michael

PS8307.S84 2009 C812'.608 C2009-903525-1

First edition: August 2009
Printed and bound by Gauvin, Gatineau

Mixed Sources
Product group from well-managed forests and other controlled sources
www.fsc.org Cert no. SGS-COC-2624
© 1996 Forest Stewardship Council
FSC

CONTENTS

INTRODUCTION

How do you adequately represent nineteen years of work in the first anthology for a theatre festival that has been a major part of the cultural design of Toronto and Canada's theatre history? That's a very large task for a very modest book! Can an anthology define an entire festival and its canon of work?

To answer this question, we must first try to understand what defines the festival itself.

Currently, the only rule is that the work has to be chosen by a jury. That's all. The artistic producer assembles a group of arts professionals to read the submitted plays and together determine whether or not the work makes sense for the festival. This is what defines SummerWorks. Or, more specifically, this is what makes SummerWorks different than, say, the Fringe Festival. Sometimes this means that the work pushes boundaries, or sometimes it means that the work is just so darn sweet that we have no choice but to include it. SummerWorks is as edgy as it is loveable. It is defined by the jury that defines it.

Of course, SummerWorks has not always been juried.

The festival began in 1991 when five friends—Benj Gallander, Greg Holmgren, Carol Pauker, Rob Sherwood, and Ben Stadelmann—all disgruntled at not getting into the Toronto Fringe, decided to start their own festival. At the time, it was not much different than the Fringe, except that it was smaller. In 2000, then-Artistic Producer Franco Boni began transitioning SummerWorks into a fully juried festival. And it's because of that transformation that SummerWorks has become one of the most important theatre festivals in the country. Each year, audiences flock to the shows because they know the quality of work will be consistently strong. It is where Toronto's theatre artists are formed. Artists like myself.

The SummerWorks Festival has been a second home to me. It helped me define myself, both as a singular voice and as a collaborative one. It is where I learned to write plays, direct plays, and sometimes do both at the same time. It is also where I developed important relationships with artists like Hannah Moscovitch, Alan Dilworth, and Franco Boni. And now, it is the place where I am learning to be an artistic and administrative leader as its artistic producer. The SummerWorks Festival gives all artists, emerging and established, a creative home—a place in which to define and redefine themselves. It is a place where an artist can take large creative risks without the burden of major financial risk. It is where a creator can feel they are a part of a larger community where the theatre is considered an important, vital artistic practice. It is a place where ambition, courage, and the pursuit of virtuosity are supported and rewarded.

This is also what defines the festival.

With all this in mind, for this anthology I chose plays that were strong but also representative of an ambitious, courageous artistic practice that the festival supports.

1. *Matador Love* and *Our Father* by Morwyn Brebner

These are two great pieces by one of Canada's most eccentric and fascinating playwrights. Many will know Morwyn for her great success with work like *Music for Contortionist* and *Little Mercy's First Murder*. What people may not know is that in 2001 Morwyn premiered these two short gems as part of the SummerWorks Festival. These plays are perfect examples of the opportunity that SummerWorks provides artists to mount work that is not able to be produced at theatres like Toronto's Tarragon or Factory. It is also significant to note that *Matador Love* was produced at the Rhubarb! Festival prior to receiving a run at SummerWorks. The SummerWorks Festival has often been a place for Rhubarb! Festival pieces to continue to grow. This relationship has, and continues to prove very important for theatre artists in Toronto.

2. *richardthesecond* by Matthew MacFadzean

I once overheard Daniel MacIvor say to Matthew MacFadzean, "Oh, you're *that* guy!" What MacIvor was referring to was the guy who did *richardthesecond*. Matthew MacFadzean is one of the most unique and unabashedly original artists in Toronto. His piece, *richardthesecond*, was a runaway hit at the SummerWorks Festival, and MacFadzean became an instant emblem for edgy SummerWorks theatre-making. His show was bold, political, and cool, and represented the kind of work young, ambitious theatre creators wanted to make. This was an important piece for the SummerWorks Festival and it's a gift to be able to include it here.

3. *Little Dragon* by Keira Loughran

Keira Loughran is one of the smartest people in theatre today. There is nothing she can't do, including writing, directing, and starring in her own piece, *Little Dragon*. This play thrust Keira and her skills into the limelight, and shortly after this piece was mounted, Keira took over the reigns as artistic producer of the festival. Three years later, Keira is now working for the Stratford Shakespeare Festival as the associate director of the Dramaturgy and New Play Department. One can only imagine where she will be heading next. She is a force to be reckoned with, and it is fitting to be able to include her play in this anthology.

4. *The Unforgetting* by Alan Dilworth

Alan Dilworth is slowly becoming one of the most exciting, important young directors in the country. He is an incredible visionary and a beautiful collaborator. *The Unforgetting* is a fantastic example of the sort of work that can come out of a strong unique and collaborative vision. It also marked a very important chapter in his work with then-collaborators Maev Beaty, Patrick Robinson, and Andrew Penner. This is a very good play that works both as a fascinating mystery and as an exploration of psychology in a very specific time and place in Canadian history.

5. *Any Night* by Daniel Arnold and Medina Hahn

Daniel and Medina (DualMinds) had a major hit with their first piece, *Tuesdays & Sundays*. It was an honour, and real cool, to have them premiere their newest work, *Any Night*, at the SummerWorks Festival. This piece was significant for the festival, as it was a part of the National Series—a series of invited work from outside of the province. It was a major success at the festival, and an example of the importance of presenting work from outside Ontario. *Any Night* is a piece created by two very ambitious artists who have set, and continue to set, an example of the rigour, intelligence, and craft that manifests successful careers in the theatre.

This anthology is representative of the great plays, great artists, and significant moments in the history of the SummerWorks Festival. Each play chosen stemmed from the juried system (2001 to the present), and are by writers who were under thirty-five at the time of creation. While SummerWorks consistently represents some of the best work this country has to offer, perhaps more poignantly, SummerWorks represents the importance of youth in creation.

I am proud to be a SummerWorks artist, proud to be the current artistic producer, and proud to have the honour of editing this publication.

—Michael Rubenfeld
Artistic Producer, SummerWorks Festival
Toronto, 2009

MATADOR LOVE

AND

OUR FATHER

BY MORWYN BREBNER

MORWYN BREBNER

Morwyn Brebner's plays include the Chalmers and Dora Award nominated *Music for Contortionist*, the musical *Little Mercy's First Murder* (winner of seven Dora Mavor Moore Awards, including outstanding new musical), and *The Optimists*, which was nominated for the 2006 Governor General's Literary Award. She was a finalist for the 2008 Elinore and Lou Siminovitch Prize. She is a graduate of the National Theatre School and a playwright-in-residence at the Tarragon Theatre in Toronto.

The summer of 2001 was incredibly hot. I remember it as the first of the freaky, global-warming summers—heat radiating up off the sidewalks. It was the year I was super skinny and wore short skirts, along with a pair of Clone heels with butterflies on the straps. I was kind of crazy then—my first play at the Tarragon had been produced to some acclaim, followed by my second, six months later, which had opened to general disappointment. *Matador Love* and *Our Father* felt like a sort of redemption.

The heat is germane. Catherine Fitch and Tony Munch, both brilliant actors and extraordinarily generous people, wore winter coats during *Our Father.* We had had fan issues at Rhubarb! the year before—i.e., the fan in the small space was so loud you couldn't hear the show—and there were similar problems with the air conditioning in the Cameron House, our SummerWorks venue. This is an intimate cabaret space with a stage the size of a cutting board. Kate Lynch, who had essentially been tricked into directing the first iteration of *Matador Love,*[1] had rightly kicked me out of rehearsal because my stress level was squelching any actual work—and by the time we got into the space, I was a basket case. But there were Catherine and Tony, acting in parkas during a heat wave. Kate had about an hour to tech the show with our stage manager, who, while very nice, was not the most accurate caller of cues. Nobody complained,

---

1 I had been looking for a director for *Matador Love* and called Kate. She actually said, "I'll read your play and think about it," but what I heard was, "Yes, I will direct your play." She called Catherine and Tony, who I didn't yet know. Now it is impossible for me to imagine these plays with other actors or in any production but Kate's.

at least not to me. They were so *good*—at their art, at managing their own stress, at staying kind while doing it. I remember watching, crouched down in the back of the theatre, by the bathrooms, where I hid like a nervous troll, thinking, these incredibly talented people are making your play. You are the luckiest woman alive. We got some great reviews (except from the *Toronto Star*'s Richard Ouzounian[2]) and the show sold out. I remember standing on the sidewalk with an extra ticket. Don McKellar was waiting in line. I thought: "I've made it."

The genesis of *Matador Love* was a phone call I had with a friend. He was more like a "friend." It was a long, combative call, during which he said, "You're like the Andy Kaufman of conversation." I had been trying to write (badly) a piece for Rhubarb! to follow up a short play called *Oh So Close* I'd written the year before. It was terrible and clunking along on square wheels until that phone call. Later I showed *Matador Love* to Urjo Kareda. At that time, the play ended with a physical fight and Urjo said, "I don't want to watch these characters hit each other." He was right, and I changed it.

Our Father has a more involved backstory. The summer before I wrote it, my two brothers and I had travelled to New Brunswick to meet our father, who was dying. The scene was so surreal—my father as described in the play, living on the top floor of an ex-girlfriend's house. We hadn't seen him since we were small children. I sat in a chair opposite him, leaving every so often to weep. My brothers sat on a couch, with all the perverse hope of orphans waiting to be picked up at the train station. Our father talked about his schemes—he was a psychic—and about the jobs he'd lost and applied for after he'd quit teaching at UNB. He read us one of his poems, which began with the line "How now, said white man to Indian chief." It was easily the strangest moment of my life and *Our Father* was my first, and so far only, attempt to write about it directly.[3]

I owe a great debt to Franco Boni, who programmed *Matador Love* at Rhubarb! then offered us a spot at SummerWorks if I could

2 Who hates my work.

3 There was a leech I saw crawling across a rock that made it into another play. And I've written a lot about my father in the unresolved way that suggests that he may be my only subject.

write a companion piece. He created a climate of total support and artistic freedom—a safe umbrella under which a writer could experiment in the heat.

—Morwyn Brebner

Matador Love was first produced as part of the Rhubarb! Festival at Buddies in Bad Times Theatre, 2001, with the following company:

ENID	Catherine Fitch
ANONYMOUS	Tony Munch

Directed by Kate Lynch

Our Father and *Matador Love* appeared as a double bill at SummerWorks in 2001 with the following company:

ENID and LILY	Catherine Fitch
ANONYMOUS and MARK	Tony Munch

Directed by Kate Lynch

MATADOR LOVE

Lights up. A restaurant. Tinny, unimposing, "romantic" music comes from somewhere. ANONYMOUS, strangely sexy, tight open shirt, maybe some chains, sits, knees spread wide, drinking his drink, idly studying the menu. ENID stands in the doorway, regarding. She wears an interesting collection of thrift store finds; not so bad. ANONYMOUS looks up, sees her.

ANONYMOUS Enid!

ENID Ah…

ANONYMOUS Enid, Enid, Enid!

ENID Hello.

ANONYMOUS Ee-nid!

ENID Hi, I'm—

ANONYMOUS You're Enid.

ENID Yeah and you're—?

ANONYMOUS *(pulling out her chair)* Sit!

ENID Uh—

ANONYMOUS Where'd you get your name, Enid? You named after a, ah, aunt?

ENID No, I'm named after, *(finally figuring out the chair thing)* thanks, Enid Blyton, who wrote the Noddy the Puppet books, y—

ANONYMOUS 'Cause you got a spinster's name there, Enid. *(sitting)* You got the name of a woman who don't have sex. Pardon my French.

ENID *(squinting hard at him)* You know… that's not *conversational*.

ANONYMOUS *(smiling)* Most women just use their initial in the phone book. "E," or "E. Something Something," never "Enid." I liked your name, in the book. It's a name you read, although it's not bad to say either: "Enid." No, it's better to read. It's a book kinda name.

ENID clears her throat, looks around.

That's how I picked you. I saw it, I thought, I'd like to phone that girl.

ENID "Phone"! "I'd like to *phone* that girl." What's that, that's like, "Didja phone her?" "Yeah, I phoned her. I phoned that hot little bitch all night." *(beat)* What are you drinking?

ANONYMOUS Gin on the rocks with a twist.

ENID That's what I'll have. *(going to signal a waiter)*

ANONYMOUS They don't have a liquor licence yet. *(showing a bottle)* Pass me your water glass, I'll do you right.

ANONYMOUS produces a large Swiss Army knife and a lemon, which he carefully peels a strip off as they talk.

ENID Normally I wouldn't do this, go on a blind date with a stranger.

ANONYMOUS All blind dates are with strangers.

ENID But you're not even a friend of a friend, you're just a— You know why? You know why I said I'd go out with you? Don't take this as an insult, I— Because I feel like, you know who I feel like? Like the Michelle Pfeiffer character in *Scarface*, when Al Pacino says, "What do you do all day? You wait for me to come home and *fuck* you!"

ANONYMOUS twists the lemon piece, drops it in the glass, pours gin on it.

I don't mean I'll fuck you, even though I might, I just mean I— Wait. I spend a lot of time in my apartment waiting. I wait and I wait. *(big, rueful drink)* So what do you do? What's your *job*?

ANONYMOUS Enid, I'm a matador.

ENID Say again?

ANONYMOUS I'm a matador. A bullfighter. I fight bulls.

ENID That's bullshit. No pun int—

ANONYMOUS No shit.

ENID Really. Are you also an "astronaut"?

ANONYMOUS Enid—

ENID Nobody's a matador! For starters, it's illegal.

ANONYMOUS There's an underground circuit.

ENID I've never heard of it.

ANONYMOUS It's *underground.*

ENID *(beyond dubious)* You fight bulls.

ANONYMOUS Mm-hm.

ENID Where? Where do you fight these alleged bulls?

ANONYMOUS In Spain, Enid, that's where I learned. Here, on farms mostly. We get sort of an informal gathering going. Start with a cockfight, hog-tie, move on up the food chain. It's not politically correct, but you know, Enid, till you've *seen* one— I nearly had something lined up at the Air Canada Centre, right? but the animal-rights people put the kibosh on that one, assholes. We were gonna throw some dirt down over the ice between periods and *do* it.

ENID So who? who? cowboys watch you fight these bulls?

ANONYMOUS Cowboys, lawyers, whoever's around.

ENID This is you: you fight bulls and you phone strange women.

ANONYMOUS You make it sound bad. Killing and uh, "phoning," what else is there?

ENID You kill the bulls?

ANONYMOUS No, I kill the women and fuck the bulls.

Beat.

ENID You think that's a romantic thing to say?

ANONYMOUS Why're you so fuckin'—

ENID You didn't even compliment my dress.

ANONYMOUS Maybe I don't like your dress.

ENID So? Isn't that the point of a date, you lie? You lie and you hope to get laid? Isn't that why people do these things?

Beat.

ANONYMOUS You look like a librarian. I know that's not romantic, it's an observation. I knew you would, Enid… look like a librarian. I knew you'd wear only lipstick, no makeup, and a cardigan. I could tell all these things from talking to you on the phone.

ENID These aren't librarian shoes.

ANONYMOUS No, ma'am, they're not. They're whore shoes.

ENID You look divorced! You look like you'd pay twice as much for those… pointy booties of yours if you didn't have alimony. What's her name?

Shannon? Sharon? Sherrie? What's she eating up? Fifty, sixty percent of your income? 'Cause you look like a guy who would have gone for *real* snakeskin. *(big drink)*

ANONYMOUS You want me to leave?

ENID It's not, it's just— Sorry, I don't, go on a lot of dates. I don't.... Some days I can't relax. I've been, ah, *(laughs)* making these fucking Pokémon watches. It's not much of an excuse for being such a cunt, *cunt!* but you know, like, piecework?

ANONYMOUS You mean like Amnesty?

ENID Piece, p-i-e-c-e. I sent away and got this fucking ginormous box of... crap, that's what it seems like, microscopic fucking pieces of Pokémon *crap*. You're supposed to put the watches together, you get, like, five cents for every watch you make, and they're toys not watches-*watches* that *work*—so I thought, you know, do it during the employment hiatus.... But it's a pig-fucker! I mean, I've made two. I've been doing this for like a month and I've made *two fucking watches*. So I've made a dime and I watch fuckin' Oprah while I'm doing it, trying to make a goddamn toy watch, Oprah for inspiration, could I be *more* pathetic, and I cannot figure it out! The watch pieces are like, are they particles or are they waves? they're *that* small! You need minimum one hundred to ship back to Japan, to get paid? By the time I make that fuckin' quota Pokémon's gonna be over, it's gonna be like—

ANONYMOUS *(making up an incomprehensible new toy)* Ggrrrgbllglkakakah!

ENID Exactly! *(drinking)* Are those spurs?

ANONYMOUS I spend a lot of time on a horse.

ENID Why? ARE YOU LIKE SOME KIND OF STEREOTYPICAL LITTLE GIRL WHO WANTS TO FUCK A HORSE!!!!

ANONYMOUS just stares at her.

I think that was a joke. But you know, when everything's a joke, how can you make a joke? I put that out there philosophically. How can you? Do you know any jokes, Matador?

ANONYMOUS Yeah. A guy phones a girl he doesn't know from her name in the white pages. She turns out to be crazy.

ENID Ha ha. I'll tell you a joke: three string walk into a bar. The bartender's like, "We don't serve string in here," so the string go outside and intertwine themselves and fluff up their top and come back in, and the bartender's like "Are you guys string?" and the string are like, "Nope, frayed knot."

Beat.

ANONYMOUS Here, *(slaps an Eat-More bar down on the table)* I brought you candy.

Beat.

ENID So.... This is a date.

Beat.

ANONYMOUS I am divorced.

ENID I am a librarian.

Beat.

ANONYMOUS What are you looking for in a man, Enid?

ENID Honestly? I'm looking for a man who's, who looks good entering a room.

ANONYMOUS Hh?

ENID Like in a movie.

ANONYMOUS Like in *Scarface*? "Say hello to my leedle—"

ENID Like Steve McQueen, like, Steve McQueen, he's entering a room, he's like, "I'm worried," he's like, "I'm packing heat and I have the weight of the world on my shoulders." He's pensive, he's pensive but he's—unh! I want a man like that.

ANONYMOUS A cop?

ENID In a movie. A cop but a movie star. Not just a lug, not a brute, but—

ANONYMOUS A tough guy. A man who carries a gun.

ENID In a movie.

ANONYMOUS A pensive guy.

ENID Right, walking into a room, contemplative.

ANONYMOUS But ready for action.

ENID Yes, yes.

ANONYMOUS *(very sincere)* Enid, I am that man.

He takes her hand.

ENID *(spit take, then)* Oh, OH!

ANONYMOUS Are you okay there?

ENID *(quietly)* I just had an orgasm.

ANONYMOUS You *came*?

ENID I think I should leave.

ANONYMOUS Stay! This is good! This is getting good! You were weird, at first, but we're establishing a, rapport here, Enid? Siddown.

ENID Can I make a confession to you?

ANONYMOUS Tell me. I can keep any secret.

ENID I've been drinking since you called me. I was incredibly nervous. I took the rest of the Valium I've been saving. I'm fucked up. I don't go on dates. I haven't been touched in years. I brush a stranger on the bus and I—I go nuts, I… it's like sex to me. Any contact. *(laughs)* A crowded street! Leaving the house is like an orgy.

He takes her hand, rolls up her sleeve, runs his fingers up the inside of her arm from her wrist to her elbow, continues stroking her wrist as he talks.

ANONYMOUS Can I tell you a confession?

ENID Mm?

ANONYMOUS This isn't a restaurant.

ENID Uhhn?

ANONYMOUS It's a location. They're shooting a movie here with Jackie Chan, and I.... It's my day job, if you can believe, I'm an actor. I'm ah, I'm playing Mr. Chan's waiter. I'm kind of, borrowing, the space here, for our date. So there's no real waiter, and there's no food. There's not gonna be any food, Enid. No food.

ENID Uhhhhh...

ANONYMOUS No food for Enid.

He lets go of her wrist, she's in a stupor. He reaches under his chair, pulls out a portable tape recorder—the source of the music—cranks it so the music swells the best it can. He goes to kiss her.

ENID Wait a, wait— Wait, a... what? This is, this is?

ANONYMOUS You wanna be touched, I'm gonna touch y—

ENID This is *moves*?!!! You're *faking* it? This is a *fake date*???

Beat.

ANONYMOUS I wouldn't say that.

ENID This isn't real? This isn't— Oh mother… mother fuck. *(beat)* Mother mother fuck your mother mother mother fucking fuck. Now you're just, like— You were all… nicey-nice, and now you're like, "She'll fuck me," so you're— *(beat, with horrible scorn) Matador*!

ANONYMOUS Hey!

ENID *Matador*! My ass, motherfucker!

ANONYMOUS Hey!

ENID Actor! Waiter! *Matador*!

ANONYMOUS Hey, fuck you!

ENID You'd be any bull's bitch in a minute!

ANONYMOUS HEY!

ENID You couldn't wrassle a fucking chicken! "Mr. Jackie Chan's waiter"!!!! Oh my God, OH MY GOD. I can't believe I let you *touch* me!

ANONYMOUS I'm a matador all right, Enid, don't you doubt that, don't you doubt me, Eni—

ENID Oh what'cha gonna do, what'cha gonna do? *(baby talking)* Is a itty-bitty matadow gonna—

He grabs her. She slaps him hard across the face.

You piece of shit. How dare you fucking pretend to be romantic with me. You think I can't get laid? Anybody can get laid! I choose not to but I *could*! I thought you were asking me on a date, you piece of shit, I thought you were—!

She slaps him harder.

You invited me on a date and *this* is the *reality* you give me???? I could *dream* this!!! I could dream this BETTER! I HAVE BETTER DREAMS THAN THIS!!! Last night I had a dream; I had a dream I went to a sex bar with some friends of mine, I don't *have* these friends, but in my dream I did and we went into like this tiny movie theatre in the sex bar behind a curtain like and the movies they were showing weren't sex movies, just movies of objects—a toaster, a lamp, *things*—but somehow everyone was incredibly turned on and suddenly I was wearing a PVC corset and this, this *woman* and I were making out, then kind of fucking around and it was SO MUCH BETTER THAN THIS!!!

She goes to slap him again, he grabs her arm.

ANONYMOUS I've been in the ring with a bull, don't tell me I can't—

ENID What, you can't, what? Because you pretend you know how to run away from a giant *cow* I'm supposed to believe you're a supernatural *lover*, a Casa—

ANONYMOUS *(warning)* Enid—

ENID —nova??? Worth this shit? Cassanova Casanova Casa—

ANONYMOUS You don't kn—

ENID —Don-Quixote-Don-Qui-Casa-fuckin'-Don-Qui-liar-mother*fucker*?!!

He slaps her; her eyes boggle, she goes to closed-fist punch him; he grabs her fist, she struggles.

You make me wish I was *dead*, people like you! Fake people, lame people, sucking real people in with your fake hearts! Like that artist from the sixties who made fake hamburgers—? You can't *eat* those! You can't *love* me! You can't *talk* to me! With your lies about yourself and your lies about everything! Lie lie lie lie, like a *rug* you lie! Like a motherfuckin' handmade fuckin' Persian rug you lie! The child labour people should find you and kill you for all the Third World children who've gone blind knotting up colourful rugs for you to *lie* with!

ANONYMOUS FUCK YOU!

ENID Oh *oh*, "*Fuck you.*" FUCK YOU!

ANONYMOUS You sanctimonious, whore-shoe bitch!

ENID Horseshoe? You wanna fuck a horsie-horse—?

ANONYMOUS Whore-shoe!

ENID *(mock you're-an-idiot incomprehension) War*-saw? Poland?

ANONYMOUS Whore-sho—

ENID *Horror show*??? Rocky *Horror Sh*—

ANONYMOUS *(grabbing her ankle, pulling the shoe from her foot, and brandishing it)* WHORE-SHOE! Jesus fucking *Christ*!

Beat. ENID teeters on one heeled foot.

Wobble there a moment while I collect myself.

Hands shaking, he replaces the tape in the tape recorder with one from his pocket, plays it: "Super Trooper" by ABBA. Wrong tape. He pulls it out, replaces it again: "Ace of Spades" by Motörhead. He cranks it—it's still sadly tinny—listens for a bit with great concentration, mouthing the occasional word, banging his head to the guitar solo, deep in thought. He looks like a little boy, strangely vulnerable. Then he turns off the tape, reels on ENID.

Okay. Okay! You wanna have a little chat? Ladies love to chat. I wish I wanted to fuck horses sometimes because *they would never want to chat*. I call you because I want a librarian type, to fuck. Okay. Anything wrong with that? I like a girl who looks like she's good with a book, comes from a porno I once saw that took place in a library. They fucked on a ladder. Maybe I have this thought in my head, you have a different one in yours. So? Honestly, I ask you, Enid, SO? You're inside your head, having your dream. I'm inside mine, having my fantasy. I touch you, you touch me, that's a lotta meat slappin' each other, you know what I'm saying? Enid? It's purely physical. Different thoughts can coexist in two very mutual moments of—

He mashes his hands together. She watches him.

ENID You don't care about me.

ANONYMOUS I don't know you!

ENID I want you to care about me.

ANONYMOUS Yeah, well...

Beat.

ENID Are you really a matador? I'm serious. I'm seriously curious.

ANONYMOUS You should have some faith.

ENID I don't have faith in anything.

ANONYMOUS You shouldn't be so doubting, Enid.

He peels off his shirt. Underneath it is a tight bolero vest. He produces a matador cap—very Mickey Mouse—out of nowhere, puts it on. It suits. Slowly the light begins to fade from the room.

Would you like to know what it's like to kill a two-ton animal, I'm talking a beast the size of a Volkswagen, with your own bare hands? Your own bare hands and a knife? Would you?

ENID I don't know if I'm interested in killing.

ANONYMOUS Bullshit. I've butchered animals, but you look like a murderess. When you walked in here I thought, you know what I thought? I thought, that's a girl who, when she's walking around, has a walk like a girl who wants to kill people.

ENID I don't want to kill anybody—thing.

ANONYMOUS Sure you do.

ENID No.

ANONYMOUS I don't believe you, Enid. I don't believe that underneath that bookish exterior there doesn't beat some kind of a… wet pulse. *(beat)* Some day I suggest you wring a chicken's neck, just to get the feel of it.

ENID You know what I think…? I think I'd like to kill *you.*

ANONYMOUS Oh yeah?

ENID Why not.

ANONYMOUS I'll give you a lesson. *(He has a firm arm around her, so he's holding her from behind.)* What you try to do is, before you make the kill, you stab the bull *here. (He touches her rib cage, probes around for the right space.)* That's what you go for, Enid, the soft spot between the ribs where you can penetrate.

His fingers deftly search out the place in her ribs. He finds the spot, pushes his fingers into it. She makes a little noise.

Now you try.

She gets behind him, arm around, with her other hand she finds a soft spot, presses. He inhales, sharp.

Not bad.

She does it again. Looks around with her eyes as the light closes in on her.

ENID Is this a dream I'm having?

ANONYMOUS You tell me.

She pushes in again. On his gasp: black.

OUR FATHER

Night. The front seat of a car. MARK drives. He wears a big parka, gloves. He could not look more pissed off. LILY sits beside him, an open map on her lap. She wears two coats, one on top of the other. From the radio, faint rap.

LILY Well, I don't know.

She traces a map line with her finger.

This looks like it. *(looking out the window)* It's wiggly.

MARK That's not helpful.

LILY I mean the line on the map is wiggly, the road outside looks w—

MARK Have you gone deaf?

LILY Fine. *(beat)* The sign a mile back said—

MARK I read it.

LILY Do you wish me to help or not?

Nothing. LILY crumples the map, unrolls the window, goes to throw it out.

MARK Please Lily, not the pointless dramatic gesture. Not right now.

MARK swerves the car onto the roadside. He turns off the ignition. Eerie silence. He lays his head gently on the steering wheel.

(in agony) Why oh why can you not drive a car!

LILY Because I'm afraid—

MARK Oh Jesus.

LILY —that I would kill someone. It's a serious fear!

MARK It's a ridiculous fear!

LILY We grew up in the city!

MARK I learned to drive!

LILY Lean over so I can pin a medal on you!

MARK *(looks outside the window)* Ah, we're fucked. Completely fucked. What do you think?

LILY I think we're on the right road. It really does look right on the map. I think we're close, we just underestimated the scale.

MARK *(very dryly)* The scale. *(looks)* I'd like to see another car right about now.

LILY We should just keep going.

MARK The gas station guy said an hour. It's been what, three? Oh I want a beer so badly.

LILY Maybe you misheard the guy.

MARK I don't think so. Listen, let's just go back.

LILY What?

MARK Let's just turn around and fuck it.

LILY After three days?

MARK That's nothing in the scheme of things.

LILY We'd regret it.

MARK I wouldn't.

LILY You would. Forever.

MARK clenches his teeth. Beat. He starts the car.

MARK *(steering back onto the road)* Sometimes I wish that life was a cartoon, you know? That a safe would fall out of the sky and flatten me. I'd be flat for a while, then rebound all springy. *(They're going at speed.)* Ah, fuck it.

Beat.

LILY Lousy visibility.

MARK Thank you. Blind drivers of North America thank you, Lily.

LILY Mark.

MARK Lily.

MARK snaps the radio off.

I need to think.

Beat.

LILY What do you think he'll look like?

MARK Like the photo.

LILY It's been twenty years. Do you think he's aged well?

MARK You mean better than Mom?

LILY I'm just curious.

MARK *(amused)* The quality of your genes. *(swerves)* Was that a porcupine?

LILY Maybe.

MARK Put on your glasses. *(She does.)* Keep an eye out for signs. I have no idea what he'll look like. Like all sick people probably. Grey and… crumpled.

LILY He sounded all right.

MARK When he called, my first thought was, he wants some bone marrow. I kept waiting for him to ask, "Can I stick a needle in your leg and suck out some marrow?"

LILY What would you have said?

MARK I dunno.

LILY I'd give it to him.

MARK With your needly paranoia? They'd have to rip off your legs to get in there.

LILY They use stem cells now anyway.

MARK From fetuses. "Feti"?

LILY Fetuses.

MARK Parents are always cannibalizing their children.

LILY Don't you have any curiosity?

MARK *(driving with concentration)* Sure, I want to see him before he dies. I'd like to see the pyramids too. I'd like to see Heather Locklear's ass in a thong. I'd like to see a lot of things.

A moment. Some kind of decisive change. MARK and LILY look out to the audience.

That was how it ended.

LILY No.

MARK You know how on a road trip time blends together and you…

LILY That wasn't how it ended. It ended when we…

MARK You can't remember what you did on any given day because it's all just one long day. In your mind, not… literally. One time I read a book about a Paraguayan dictator. It was reminiscence—a fake one, a fictional book like—about his life.

LILY Since he read *Moby Dick* he's all like, with books.

MARK (*over her*) It was called *Yo El Supremo.* I read it in English but the title wasn't translated.

LILY Mark, that's not nearly where it ended. That might be where we stopped talking, but—

MARK And it was, when you were reading it, like it took place over the course of one long day. The dictator was dying, reminiscing. It was his entire life, but: it was told from his minion's point of view. Even though the dictator was a total asshole, his minion loved him. It's always the minion who survives to tell the story of the great man.

LILY Mark.

MARK The minion reminiscing over the course of one long day. On the road it was like that. Right?

LILY (*giving up*) Sure.

MARK So.

BOTH Earlier.

Black. The strains of the beginning of the Ol' Dirty Bastard album N***a Please. *Lights up. MARK drives. LILY bounces in the seat beside him to the beginning of "Got Your Money." They wear coats but don't seem cold.*

LILY Not bad.

MARK I don't wanna talk about it.

LILY You left them on what, the kitchen counter.

MARK Shut up.

LILY We could stop at Canadian Tire and buy some new ones.

MARK What, Bryan Adams?

LILY Or we could go back. It's only like, a hundred miles.

MARK You wanna hitchhike home?

LILY *(savouring his mistake)* So, this is our only CD. Could be worse.

MARK Maybe we'll get some radio.

LILY You haven't driven cross-country very much. I don't know about down East, but out West, country, country, and more country. You pray for like, "Jump," by Van Halen.

MARK That's a great song!

LILY I guess. You know what the best song is?

MARK *(drolly)* "Islands in the Stream"?

LILY No, driving song. "Turn Me Loose" by Loverboy.

MARK Are you fuckin' serious?

LILY When I moved to Toronto, we were coming down off the highway, like three in the morning, almost no traffic, it had been a total nightmare, the futon got untied from the roof and nearly caused a school bus to, and, anyway all kinds of shit, Shel—

MARK Shel!

LILY Shut up!

MARK What a chump!

LILY Shel and I weren't talking to each other and, what I'm saying is, we turned off the freeway onto the off-ramp and at that instant the radio got a signal and "Turn Me Loose" came on and.... You know! Fuckin' "Turn Me Loose," man! It was just perfect. A perfect moment.

MARK *(nods)* Yeah. When Mike Reno... *(sings the last, crescendo-y line before the chorus)* Fuck.

LILY Metal!

MARK That's not really metal.

LILY Still.

MARK You gotta love metal

LILY You know what the best metal thing is?

MARK After Sabbath? Lee Aaron singing "Metal Queen." *(sings)*

LILY *(over him)* David Lee Roth saying "I got what you need."

MARK Fuck, for sure.

LILY You know he's not talking about affordable housing. Hey.

MARK What?

LILY I'm so glad you agreed to come. It would have been horrible to do it alone. I know you don't like to travel and I… I'm so glad you're here.

MARK sort of nods. He cranks up the stereo. It's bright.

MARK Hand me my shades.

She does. He puts them on.

***

Afternoon. MARK drives. He has the window open, elbow propped out. LILY eats Cheezies from a bag.

LILY Do you think he's really psychic?

MARK No.

LILY He thinks he's for real.

MARK He's a charlatan.

LILY But that's the thing: if he believes he's for real, even if he's not, does that make him a faker?

MARK If I tell you I'm a doctor, and I'm not, even if I believe I am, and I perform open-heart surgery on you, and you die because I have no idea what I'm doing, is it malpractice?

LILY You can't kill people reading their futures.

MARK He's a scam artist.

LILY I don't think so. I think he thinks he has a gift.

MARK "The gift."

LILY What would you call it?

MARK Bullshit.

LILY Sometimes I think I'm a psychic.

MARK You should ask him to leave you the business.

LILY I'm serious.

MARK What number am I thinking of?

LILY Seven.

MARK Nope.

LILY Four.

MARK Twenty-three.

Beat.

LILY My therapist thinks I'm a sex addict because I didn't have a father.

MARK I don't want to know about—

LILY I didn't have the proper grounding so I think all men are accessible.

MARK *(pronouncing for similarities)* Psychiatrist… psychic. From the Latin for bullshit.

LILY You should see one.

MARK Yeah I probably should. You know what, Lily? Drop it.

LILY What like I could never, I could never have good advice?

MARK *(pointing to the Cheezies)* Hey, aren't those hydrogenated?

LILY What?

MARK Hydrogenated fat. I thought you were worried about getting breast cancer from free radicals.

LILY You think I'm a simpleton, don't you. That you can just point and say "Look over there!" and I'll be so distracted I'll lose my train of thought. Listen, you should see a psychiatrist because you have a very deep-seated, repressed anger.

MARK Oh God, here we go.

LILY You're so angry you can't even get angry. It's like magma, boiling away somewhere hidden.

MARK "Magma."

LILY You hate him for leaving you, fatherless, stuck with Mom, the whole nine yards.

MARK You know what Lily, I don't even know the guy.

LILY — You hate him so much you can't acknowledge it without being overwhelmed, so it comes across as indifference.

MARK — *(suddenly pointing)* Hey! Look over there!

To his satisfaction, she does.

***

Late afternoon. MARK belches loudly.

LILY — Oh!... Do you gotta—?

MARK — *(innocently)* What?

LILY — You know, you're vile. Totally—

MARK belches again.

Ah! Do you, do you always do that?

MARK — Sure.

LILY — Angela must like it.

MARK — She loves it. It's why she married me.

LILY — Do you think you'll have, you know, children?

MARK — Maybe in a while.

LILY — *(a little wry)* You're so normal now.

MARK — Damn straight. From fuck-up to fly-right.

LILY *(squinting)* I don't think I've ever spent this much time with you before. Ever.

MARK When we were kids.

LILY No, not… alone. Not like, I mean…. One of us always lived away.

MARK I guess that's true.

LILY You lived with the Millers, and I was in and out, and then Malcom left home and…. You moved back and I was gone. I guess, the munchkins, they were always there.

MARK Ah, the munchkins. Do you think they resent being shorter?

LILY They resent being younger.

MARK I'd rather have our father then the munchkins' father.

LILY Any day.

MARK Our father, for all of his faults, is the superior father.

LILY *(snorts)* Yeah. Poor munchkins. *(beat)* Did he ever like, did he ever send you things?

MARK Our father?

LILY Mm.

MARK Like what things? The lame gifts?

LILY No, I mean letters.

MARK Why would he send me letters?

LILY He sent me letters.

MARK He sent you letters?

LILY Well, I sent him letters first.

MARK Oh.

LILY But then I… stopped writing. He was just so… impersonal. He just told me about his stupid business ideas, or—

MARK Like what?

LILY He was going to go into the Indian head massage business.

MARK Jesus.

LILY It was a franchise out of Bombay.

MARK *(snorts, remembering) The Complete Works of Edgar Allan Poe.* What kind of present is that for a little kid?

LILY That was really the year he sent stuff, wasn't it. Did you ever read that book?

MARK *(nods)* I'm still afraid of being buried alive.

LILY And I got a Moosehead beer T-shirt. Those were the days. His gifts sucked.

MARK They were better than welfare presents.

LILY No kidding. Perfume samples. Why did they always put those in the bag?

MARK Sears threw'em out.

LILY What the fuck kid wants a crack-vial-sized tester of Paco Rabanne for Christmas?

Beat.

MARK What were the letters about?

LILY Nothing, I guess. I would say, "School is going like X," and he would write back in answer to the questions I had. "Are you really a psychic?" "Do you have any other children?"

MARK Does he?

LILY Not that he knows of. Apparently. *(tries to wring coffee out of the bottom of a spent cup)* I don't know, the whole exercise was depressing. He never volunteered anything, you know, of significance. I would ask and ask and after a while I thought, why is all the onus on me?

MARK He's a fucking asshole.

LILY What do you think it would've been like if they'd stayed together.

MARK Horrible.

LILY Do you really think? If he'd kept teaching instead of…

MARK Going crazy? They're both crazy, that's the problem.

LILY You think she's crazy?

MARK She's fucking nuts.

LILY What do you think it's like to have regular parents?

MARK *(sort of laughs)* Why torture yourself? Why worry about the… metaphysics.

LILY You don't think you missed out?

MARK Lily, you're scratching a scab. Anyway, how can you "miss out" when you don't— What I'm saying is, I can't miss things I don't know about. I didn't "miss out" on growing up rich, for instance, because it's just another reality I don't know about.

LILY But you know of the advantages you would have accrued—

MARK No. You *miss* a lost pet. You can't miss something you never had. If I'd known him and then he left, maybe I'd miss him. You see what I'm saying?

LILY But don't you in any way intuitively feel like you missed out?

MARK No.

LILY I feel—

MARK Lily.

LILY I feel such a sense that I'm missing something. Like when my wisdom tooth was taken out. I didn't need it, but I still feel like it should be there. I keep it in a box, you know. My tooth.

MARK rolls his eyes.

(really pushing) Don't you feel like if they'd stayed together maybe—

MARK You know what, it probably would have been great. Ball games, dinner on the table. Driving around in the back of a station wagon. Getting an allowance. Being fucking told what to do once in a while. Being… brought up. Being normal. "I got an A!" "Hey Dad, how do you long divide?" "Hey Mom and Dad, my school play's on Friday." Yeah, it would've been great.

LILY Are you being sarcastic?

MARK I don't know.

Beat.

LILY She never came to anything of mine.

MARK I didn't want her at any of my things. And I'm not thrilled with him suddenly showing up and… fucking up the program.

LILY I like other people's fathers.

MARK Oh yeah?

LILY Not in that way. I just like to be around… fatherliness.

MARK "Fetch me my slippers."

LILY Exactly.

Silence as they both contemplate happily.

***

MARK is getting into the car. He looks traumatized.

LILY Did you get me my Coke?

MARK *(like a scared autistic boy)* U-uh, u-uh, u-uh—

LILY What? Are you o—?

MARK That bathroom. So filthy. There was a… a giant… log of shit in the toilet that looked like… King Kong's hand, it was…

He demonstrates, shudders audibly. Black just as LILY cracks up.

***

The radio is cranked. "Turn Me Loose" by Loverboy plays. It's getting into the chorus. They sing along, ending with the high note. So joyful.

***

Night. LILY sleeps. MARK drives, tired. So sick of the ODB, he clicks off the CD and listens to the static silence.

***

Blindingly sunny. They both wear shades. LILY unwraps a hamburger for MARK, hands it to him. She lays out fries on her lap.

LILY Pierre Trudeau.

MARK I've always said that. Magnum P.I.

LILY Definitely. The Bob Fosse character in *All That Jazz.*

MARK A speed addict who dies at the end of a movie?

LILY We would know how to dance.

MARK Reveen the Mentalist.

LILY *(sings)* The Man, the man they call Reveen.

MARK The father in *Bewitched*, what was his name?

LILY Darrin? Maybe that was *I Dream of—*

MARK Him too. Any of the old-school dads.

LILY Neil Young.

MARK Nah, his kids have birth defects.

LILY Really.

MARK Mm-hum. I met a guy, when Ange and I were in Hawaii, whose job was painting Neil Young's house on the Kona coast.

LILY Really?

MARK No joke. It was a permanent full-time job. Neil would hate everything and they'd have to redo. This guy Mike, the painting guy, would be like *(stoner voice)* "I used to love Neil, man. Now I just like, I *hate* him." Neil and him and a giant Samoan guy slaving away painting the underside of the porch. Anyway, Neil's kids have a, some kind of brain thing. The house has elevators 'cause they're in chairs. *(eats)* Mm, Hendrix.

LILY *(laughs)* Babar.

MARK The elephant?

LILY Hey, he was a good father. Don't you love this sky?

MARK *(noncommittal)* Mm.

LILY The "Voice of God" sky. You know, big clouds and a beam of sun shooting through. "This way!" I could almost believe, looking at a sky like this.

MARK In God?

LILY Do you believe in God?

MARK *(scoff)* No. Do you?

LILY No. Do you remember when we stopped going to church?

MARK Sure. She was so irate.

LILY I just didn't believe. It seemed like such a sham.

MARK I was in it for the snacks. Juice and cookies afterwards.

LILY The United Church!

MARK What a fake church!

LILY How can grape juice be a sacrament? You were too young to have to do Sunday school but I remember sitting there while whatsisface, the guy who became a Scientologist, explained how *Star Wars* was really the story of Jesus. At the end of every class we had to look the person on our right in the eye and say "Let the force be with you."

MARK crumples his wrapper, shoots it into the back seat. Suddenly pointed.

MARK Did you steal money from Mom?

LILY No.

MARK Tell the truth, Lily.

LILY No.

MARK You did.

LILY Well, maybe once.

MARK You did it all the time.

LILY What was I supposed to do!

MARK Fuck. I knew it! I always took the rap for you. Always.

LILY I'm sorry.

MARK Apologies Lily, but in some ways you were a horrible sister.

LILY I said I'm sorry!

MARK You'd act so good then.... The minute she wasn't looking you were smoking, stealing, drinking.... All the things I got caught for.

LILY Well you got to have fun at least. You weren't mothering the munchkins.

MARK You were such a martyr.

LILY You were a brat.

MARK At least I wasn't a hypocrite.

LILY Hypocrisy keeps you from getting caught.

MARK No kidding.

LILY Remember when you went to jail for being high?

MARK Fuck yeah. The cops just picked me off the side of the road.

LILY When they came to the door, I couldn't stop laughing. The thought of you in a cell all pissed off and stoned. Mom was so stupid. She just cried at the cops. She couldn't even go down to get you out. *(beat)* I guess that's not a funny story. I wasn't a very good sister. It's true. I never protected you.

MARK You couldn't have done anything anyway.

LILY I never really helped you.

MARK Don't worry about it.

LILY You turned out so well. Better than me.

MARK You're fine. Impecunious, but fine.

LILY *(routinely defensive)* It's hard to make a living playing the recorder.

MARK At least you're doing what you want.

LILY Did you think, when you were young, that that's what you would do?

MARK Ah, I just wanted to skateboard around and get high.

LILY Can you believe we're adults?

MARK Not really.

Beat.

LILY What do you think he'll be like?

MARK Our father?

LILY Yeah.

MARK You keep asking that.

LILY You won't answer.

MARK Because I don't know.

Beat.

LILY This is the sky. The V.O.G. sky. Have you noticed that, how crazy the clouds have been lately? They've been weird. Seriously. Chocking up everything. Then they part and it's like you're an ant being fried with a giant magnifying glass.

Beat.

He called us, Mark, and we got in the car and started to drive.

MARK I started to dri—

LILY Why?

MARK Because you bullied me into it.

LILY He's our father.

MARK He's just a guy. A stranger.

LILY He's our father anyway.

MARK What does it matter?

LILY I don't know. But I feel that it does.

MARK The past only matters if you keep obsessing over it.

LILY That's not true. Everybody's past is part of their present.

MARK *(grins)* That's tautology.

LILY No it's not.

MARK *(sanguine)* I like to believe that the past is behind me.

LILY That's what I just said.

MARK Nun uh. Behind me. And if you look back, you end up like Lot's wife.

LILY *(sarcastic)* Salty?

MARK Fuck off.

LILY You can't ignore the circumstances that made you.

MARK Nothing made me. I made myself.

LILY That's impossible.

MARK And yet, it is. If you look at it your way, Lily, that bastard ruined my life in advance.

LILY *(quietly)* I don't mean predestination.

MARK *(bizarrely cheerful but vehement)* If you look at it your way, Lily, my fatherless fucking life was over before it started. I was doomed. Doomed to be insecure. To walk like a girl for lack of role models. To be lacking in general. To be sad. Do you believe that, Lily?

LILY No.

MARK My house, my wife, my life. These are good things, Lily.

LILY Stop saying my name so much.

MARK So we'll meet him. Then he'll die. And you know what?

LILY Mark.

MARK Nothing will have changed.

LILY I feel nauseous, stop the car. I'm not joking.

He does. She practically falls out the door, retching. MARK gets out, paces as she vomits. LILY finishes. She finds a napkin in the car, wipes her mouth.

Oh fuck.

MARK What.

LILY The sun is gone. Oh God. What do you think he'll be like?

MARK I don't know.

LILY *(Looking away, quiet and fiercely.)* I hope he'll be like you.

***

LILY *(to the audience)* It wasn't the sunny day. It was the last night when I threw up. Driving on the windy old highway into that tiny town.

MARK It was the last day. It was the last day she threw up. It was night, and it was the last day. And after that, we didn't talk.

He looks away.

LILY The next day on the way back?

MARK That's when I threw up.

LILY But we met him.

MARK That's fucked up. To have your first meeting with your father be your last.

LILY I barely remember anything about being in the room with him.

MARK He sat in a chair, facing us.

LILY We sat together on a couch.

MARK The room was at the top of a house.

LILY Not his house. A woman's.

MARK He wore a Guatemalan fez to cover the hole in his head where they poured the chemo.

LILY Our older brother Malcom was there.

MARK The room had a bright light.

LILY It was sunny. You could swim in the lake.

MARK The town only had about fifty people in it.

LILY At the inn where we stayed they said, "How are you related to him?"

MARK Nobody knew he had children.

Beat.

Our father. Who art in heaven.

***

Sitting in the car. Sitting in the car. Sitting in the car. Black.

RICHARDTHESECOND

BY MATTHEW MACFADZEAN

MATTHEW MACFADZEAN

Matthew MacFadzean makes his living as an actor and writer, having written and produced eight of his own pieces, including *Danespotting*, *Moon Stories*, and *richardthesecond*. His work has appeared in Toronto, Montreal, and as far away as Spain and Singapore. His most recent project, *The Mill*, will have its premiere at the Young Centre for the Performing Arts in Toronto in the autumn of 2009. He lives in Parkdale, a neighbourhood in Toronto, with his dog, Connor.

I had someone say to me recently that you get three big breaks in life. Three times life turns you around a corner and there you are with a new wonderful you, and you are elevated to a new personal pinnacle. This is the kind of phrase I never forget and then tend to live by, much to the chagrin of my life, which then becomes about waiting for the next one, or looking back and counting only one big break so far. And it was *richardthesecond*. Yes, its success did a number of nice things for me professionally, but much, much more so, I learned a huge deal about myself from the experience.

I don't want this to be a rambling essay about finding oneself as an artist, we all live our own experience of that, but it must be mentioned that *richardthesecond* had a great deal to do with finding myself as an artist. I first performed it at the Montreal Fringe, where I'd performed a number of shows before, and wanted to use it as a bit of a testing ground for the piece to see how well it worked. Before the opening performance, I left the stage and went to the bathroom, took off all my clothes, looked in the mirror, and dripped with sweat. Again, I feel it important to note that this wasn't some artistic look in the mirror moment, I thought I was dying and was trying to see straight: I've never felt stage fright like that before or since. I couldn't do the show. Not a chance. Somehow I hadn't realized that doing a one-man show about something I feel absolutely passionate about would involve getting in front of people all by myself and letting them know how I feel. Hello world, this is how Matthew MacFadzean feels. I hadn't realized the intimacy such a show would demand of my politics. I've always admired stand-up comedians for their balls to go up in front of strangers and assume they're funny. What I did felt similar.

Of course I went and did the show, and luckily it was terrible, because that forced me to take the month before SummerWorks and rewrite. And that's what I did. And then one night I was out at a rave, very high, and I watched a really friendly looking girl sit down with a really friendly looking boy. She smiled at him, took his hand, and there they sat watching people dance, never once saying a word to one another. I really don't know what it was about that moment, but I immediately ran home and rewrote the whole play, beginning to end. I wrote all through the night until four p.m. the following afternoon. I printed it out and called a dear friend of mine and told her I was coming over to give her the play. I told her I was about to get on a plane to go on holiday, and if that plane crashed, this was the play to be produced; this was it, these were the words, it was done, here it is, okay, take it. I love the guy that did that. I love what that mania meant. I love also that I knew then I'd gotten it right. In the opening credits I dedicate the show to the girl at the club who gave me the hit of e that opened me up to the idea. Her name was Susie. I have no idea who she is.

I've had a theatre career for over a decade now, been acting and writing forever, but the thing is (sshhhh) I'm not a great fan of the art form. At its worst, I find it boring, unstimulating, and most often condescending. Why can't theatre be stimulating? Why can't it appeal to my generation? Why can't it have as many bells and whistles as television or film? My thinking is that it must compete if it is going to survive this age of film and TV domination, that it must move forward and divorce itself from the antique. Look at the audience that goes to the theatre. Compare their blue-rinse bills with those of the people watching TV or going to the movies and you understand how much theatre is merely nostalgia, a swan song for an age of art long gone.

But wait! Isn't that exactly the point? Theatre's the most primal form we have! Theatre can do all these things that TV and film cannot! And actually, that's true! Theatre can take place in the mind. It is a metaphysical art that gets confused and twisted into being a presentational art. At its best, it should display *ideas*, not necessarily *stories*. Film and TV whoop theatre's butt in terms of storytelling; but theatre can present you with an empty space, and we all recognize that empty space as us, and then anything that enters that empty space we interpret not as a person, but as a thought. Good theatre connects us to something inside we've somehow always known but never spoke, triggers it, and never lets us forget it ever again. But most theatre seems to tell me how to think. It will always be wrong. Because I don't think the way that that writer thinks. And neither do you. You think your way. Plant the seed. And trust that I, as audience, will water it with *my* experiences, because *my* comparative experience will affect me on a far deeper level than *yours* ever could. All this to say I set out to do something relevant, stimulating, and dangerous that would scare you for reasons personal to you. I knew my writing wasn't anything like what makes A Great Play. I hope it never is.

SummerWorks gave me a chance to do all this. I had a team of excellent people (who I still feel indebted to to this day) help me build an extremely difficult show, especially in the context of a summer festival. We had film, a DJ, computers, screens, all that stuff that is not a good idea when you've got fifteen minutes of set-up time. And I'm very proud to say we rocked it. It was one of the most incredible experiences of my life. Big Break Number One. I stood up there and told people how I felt about some important issues in a way that people found entertaining. It was hugely empowering and taught me that I can and, more importantly, *must* continue to challenge myself artistically, personally, and most of all, spiritually. Doing *richardthesecond* made me understand what was at stake: if I call myself an artist, I must speak my mind; that is the deal. From editing to computers to the countless personal mistakes I made with co-workers to rewrites to rehearsals, etc., I realized, or rather was reminded, once again, that satisfaction comes from learning, not success. And the learning curve was so big on this show, and worth all the sweat and tears and fears. I also learned that if you ever do a show in (what was) Artword and it involves transmitting signals from the booth to the stage, you will actually broadcast a Punjabi radio station. This can be fixed.

The show did well, won the SummerWorks prize, and went on to play three more times: once in the backspace at Passe Muraille, once at Harbourfront as part of the HATCH festival, and once at the newly renovated Al Green Community Centre, where we did it for high-school kids, my first and only experience doing a show for kids. Here is what I learned from that: inner-city kids are beautiful and brilliant and fascinating. Here is what I had forgotten: private-school kids are pricks. But SummerWorks was the launching pad. SummerWorks is where it found itself, and I did too to a great extent. SummerWorks allows pieces to be in a raw enough form that shows can succeed purely out of the passion of their actors or the scope of their ambition; theatre elsewhere, for obvious reasons, is likely more polished and less edgy. That's okay too, it's just different. In fact, one complaint I heard from some after seeing *R2* outside of SummerWorks was that they preferred it at the festival for exactly that reason: it was rawer. I often suggest to people with new work to "try it out at SummerWorks" because it's a great venue to express something at its most honest, at a point in its development where passion rules and your brain hasn't messed it up with dangerous words like "form" and "structure." SummerWorks isn't about making money (is theatre ever?); SummerWorks is about putting it out there, it's about taking a risk, it's about seeing what happens: these are all exciting things. What differs between SummerWorks and the Fringe is that SummerWorks doesn't have a lot of idiots who just want to do a play: all the folks I ever met at SummerWorks have always been pretty committed to doing something great. That's a great community to hang with for a couple of weeks, if not for eternity. And sometimes, a show can get enough critical notice that it can have a life elsewhere. This is always good news.

When we did the show at TPM, it was in its best shape. It had been tested, tightened (script, performance, tech), and the space was also better suited to the show. I had moved from complete and utter fear of what I was saying to claiming these opinions as my own. I grew up. And sadly, I felt it. The show became less relevant. And so did I. *R2* was very *No Logo* in its themes, and in the few years of it being performed, we as a society moved through those ideas, and once that happens it becomes mainstream, taken for granted, a given, and not much of anything to shout about. I could feel it losing its grasp of the zeitgeist as productions moved forward. I've been asked if I'd ever do the show again and I always say: "What for?" It's over. And it is. It's no longer relevant. It hit the sense of a moment. People responded. And they wouldn't now. They *shouldn't* now. They should change the channel. And get on with what affects them *now.*

Since the show was put on the shelf, much of my relationship with theatre has been about acceptance. *R2* concerned itself with an overstimulated culture, and we certainly live in one; hell, I love living in one, and I needed to accept that. I love our culture so much that a time came when I had to accept that theatre itself, the pace of it, the thrust of it, moves too slow for my liking. *R2* was also highly visual and I had to accept that I preferred visual mediums, and unfortunately, mainstream theatre is currently a medium of words. So in a way, it's interesting that a young guy writing about the barrage of images we face each day and the cost of such a barrage would then go marching happily towards it. I accept now that the show came about as much due to my fear of television as because of my absolute love of it. All this was pretty easy to accept. I am a TV person. Even now, as I am about to mount a project now called *The Mill*, I am influenced by television. With *The Mill* I set out to create a "serial for the stage," a four-part "miniseries" using the same characters throughout, tracing an arc of a story over four parts. Basically this is using a television model for the stage, with the hopes (once again) of drawing a TV audience into the theatre. And once that's done? Well. I feel I am soon to come upon my Second Big Break. But that first one was the coolest. That first one was the rawest. I was a younger man. And I claimed how I feel about the world. And I won't ever turn back.

—Matthew MacFadzean

PLAYWRIGHT'S NOTE

I am a great lover of Shakespeare, as many of us are, and am always struck with how neatly the plays of Shakespeare seem to fit into different periods of history. *Henry V* is commonly linked to nationalism, *Richard III* to dictatorship, et cetera… or often the spirit of a play mirrors the spirit of an age: when we are power hungry we are Macbeth, when we are impetuous we are Romeo and Juliet, when we are naive we are Othello, when we are lost we are Lear. When we are ineffectual we are Richard II.

And so I set out to create a modern Richard, whom I feel encapsulates the time in which we are presently living. Shakespeare wrote Richard as a dreamer more than a king, a tad cocky, a bit of a whiner, not much of a leader, and destined to fall from the get-go: certainly not suited for kingship or any position of authority. We watch him make a number of poor choices, political and otherwise, and then it's not long before the results of these bad decisions come back to get him. His crown is usurped, he is put in prison, and then murdered. The end. But what is interesting about Richard is his eloquence of language and his ability as a thinker. As the play progresses and he begins his fall, Richard becomes more and more self-aware, dissecting his lot in life of being placed on earth as the king who shouldn't be king. He is a tragic character, at times even pathetic, but we always admire him for his insight.

I see our present age as a terribly irresponsible one, particularly over here in the McWest. As witnessed by the impending environmental shutdown we are pushing to get to, it seems we are a race desperate to get onto the next big thing, the next sequence of buttons. We don't take the time to look back at the past or consider future consequences: if it's bigger and faster, that's good; if our children don't know wild animals, that's runoff. We can go to Mars... but we can't talk to each other. Human connection is becoming obsolete as our technology advances; we are evolving past it. And that's too bad. It's too bad that something like the theatre could become extinct because we don't "need" human connection. We *do* need live interaction. We *do* need theatre. We need Shakespeare to teach us about the spirit of our age. As the "leaders" of this planet, are we, like Richard, perhaps ill-suited to our charge? Is this an age of awaiting deposition? And by whom?

—Matthew MacFadzean, 2001

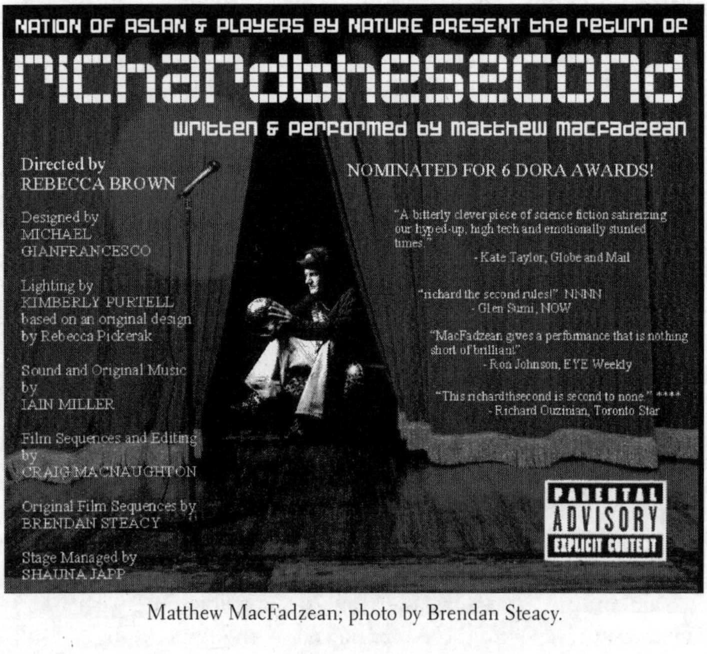

Matthew MacFadzean; photo by Brendan Steacy.

richardthesecond was first produced at the Festival St. Ambroise Fringe de Montreal and at the SummerWorks Theatre Festival in June and August 2001, with the following company:

Written and performed by Matthew MacFadzean
Directed by Rebecca Brown
Stage managed by Natasha Mytnowych
Production consultation by Dana Osborne
Sound and original music by Iain Miller
Film sequences by Brendan Steacy
Edited by Rich Gagne
Visual effects by Collon Brown

Featuring David Francis as GENE

With: Jennifer Engels, John Price, Marie-Jose Levebvre, Julius Chapple, Imali Perara, Lori Delorme, Michelle Winters, Gord Rand, Craig Erickson, Nicole Pillar, Cyrus Lane, Brendan Steacy, Wendy MacFadzean, Noam Rosen, Ha Chu, Ian Hart, and the Buyak brothers.

Subsequent performances were mounted at the Theatre Passe Muraille Backspace, October 10–27, 2002, and at the Harbourfront Studio Theatre, December 2–7, 2003, with the following company:

Same as above, but with the following changes:

Lighting design by Rebecca Picherack
Set design by Michael Gianfrancesco
Film sequences and editing by Craig MacNaughton
Original film sequences by Brendan Steacy
Stage managed by J.P. Robichaud

With: Jennifer Engels, Jennifer Gerlach, Cathy Gordon-Marsh, Ian Hart, Christina Jol, Marie-Josée Lefebvre, Chris McCawley, Cameron MacDuffee, Wendy MacFadzean, Craig Erickson, Nicole Pillar, Michelle Polak, John Price, and the Buyak brothers.

A further performance was mounted at the Al Green Theatre, October–November 2003, with the following company:

Same as above, but with the following changes:

Lighting design by Kimberly Purtell (based on an original design by Rebecca Picherack)
Stage managed by Shauna Japp
Technical direction by Trevor Schwellnus

STAGING NOTES

Please note that there are instances in the play that involve punctuation that is intentionally not gramatically correct. These are intended to supply rhythm. For instance, "of. when. i. was." contains periods that are meant to create a light staccato sense to the phrase, rather than full stops between each word.

A large screen hangs on the upstage wall.

There could be more than one screen. More and big and loud is generally a rule here. We did a couple of productions with two screens (the original version was done with five TV sets), but in the end we preferred the symmetry of the single screen.

Stage right is a television set.

Centre stage is a white chair, facing upstage. It sits on a revolve. Slumped in the chair is a figure in a baseball cap, hoodie, and flares, presumably asleep in front of the TV. In one hand is a toy lightsabre.

Surrounding the space is a white perimeter light box.

Only one production was done with the DJ and stage manager in the booth. Having them visible to the audience is interesting, and lends to the themes, but not necessary.

Pop-culture updates, however, are very necessary. Help yourself.

PROLOGUE

As the audience is entering, the screen shows the "no signal" signal, those horizontal stripes seen when a channel is out of service. On top of that reads: "This is what's on TV after it rains and the sun comes out."

At five minutes before time, Eminem's "Without Me" starts and the horizontal stripes are manipulated to move up and down like an equalizer level thingame.

After the track is done, the screen starts flipping channels, surfing through early morning television programs. The word "OVERTURE" *is superimposed on top. We hear the overture. We are now beginning our programming day.*

At time, "OVERTURE" *fades out, the flipping channels end, the music is gone, the house lights dim. The stage is black. We are waiting.*

Here we go.

A *note:* BWAAAAAAA.

Long pause.

Again: BWAAAAAA, deep n daunting, like some massive tech-anthem is about to unfold.

First we hear a cough, followed by some papers rustling.

And then a voice. GENE.

GENE Diversity… is… necessary. *(cough)*

This repeats, still all in black, and eventually we realize it is repeating to the rhythm. This goes on a while until GENE*'s voice again:*

In 1859, Charles Darwin publishes *The Origin of the Species*, outlining his theory of natural selection.

And another BWAAAA: tension escalating.

In 1866, George Mendel publishes his work on plant heredity. This work is largely ignored until the early twentieth century, when his findings become the basis for modern genetics.

Un autre, s'il vous plait. *Bring it.*

In 1883, Darwin's cousin, Francis Galton, coins the word "eugenics," in essence turning natural selection into an applied science. The universe is getting smaller.

One more, one more, I can take it:

The Nazis apply eugenics to human beings, turning "cleansing" into a dirty word.

Oh talk to me:

By the mid-sixties, biochemists decipher the genetic code. We. understand. DNA. God is officially dead.

Damn.

The early seventies sees research perfecting the first commercial uses of genetic engineering.

By now the beat has, of course, intensified to a maximum… it kicks out and…

The screen flips on. We see a man lying in bed, sick, dying. His name is GENE. He is a scientist. This is his deathbed. We have been listening to his last will and testament… which he is trying to videotape. He holds a stack of paper in one hand and a video camera converter in the other.

In this pause in music, he says:

Star Wars is released.

Boom. The tune finally kicks in. We now have a slow-throbbing spot on the throne onstage, which has begun to revolve around to face the audience. The figure is having a nightmare, getting worse by the moment. The shot cuts to GENE, yelling off, presumably to a nurse:

THE "ON" BUTTON. WHERE IS IT?

Jump-cut to GENE, pointing the converter down the barrel of the camera.

On on on on…

He coughs.

Jump-cut again to GENE, staring blankly into the camera. He has no idea it is turned on. He squints.

Jump-cut again to GENE, grumbling away to himself, banging the converter:

Hi-tech hoo-ha.

Jump to GENE, as before, with the remote pointing at the camera, still trying to find the "on" button.

On on on on…

Jump to GENE, as before, shouting off to a nurse:

THE "ON" BUTTON. WHERE IS IT?

He coughs.

He finds it.

WHAT? NO. No, I got it.

The tunes shift up a notch.

Jump to GENE, same shot as before, staring into the camera. Is it on? He squints. Coughs.

Jump to GENE, addressing the camera, now nearing the end of his speech, almost teary he is so full of regret:

It is... unavoidable: we move forwards. That's what we do.

The film loops.

That's what we do.

And loops again:

That's what we do.

And again:

That's what we/what/what/what we do/ We move f/f/f/f/f/forwards/ We move forwards/ That's what we do/ We move forwards/ We move/ We move forwards/ That's what/move/

Cut to close on his face, maybe tears now:

My God.

BAM. A disco ball falls from the ceiling into the figure's hand. The lightsabre is his sceptre. The image of royalty. He is... RICHIE EXCELLENT. *And like Hannibal Lecter attached to that trolley, or Stephen Hawking in his wheelchair,* RICHIE *has been brought to us. And we are lucky for it. He awakens with a:*

RICHIE *STOP!*

RICHIE *is looking at us, waking, remembering that we would be here. Considering... something. And it makes us slightly uneasy.*

But wait... a wee bit more on our new best friend, RICHIE EXCELLENT. RICHIE is what we could call a "mature" clubber. Not a raver or anything neon-pacifier-whistle-like (in fact, he frowns on that crap), but rather one of the sophisticates, one of the inner sanctum. One of those who has done the scene for years and still keeps a toe in the water, two steps ahead of trends. Hell, he sets the trends. And he knows this. Which makes him a culture snob. It's that fine line these types ride between massive indifference and opinionated-to-a-fault. In another era, he's the young intellectual playboy, the Byron, with silk robe, pipe, and topless, full-figured women lying about. But since this is 2000-whatever and "wits" no longer exist as a form, he remains... something of a cocky prick. The consummate reefer-roller. Smart and he knows it. The coolest of the cool. He knows it. And we love him: the stoned-psychotic-cerebral stand-up-comic.

An odd pause, and then:

Thanks for making the long drive out, I know there were other parties n shit. You will be remembered. Welcome. Make yourself at home, it's a little messy, pretty low-fi, just a television and this chair that doesn't look comfy at first, but then you find that it's like completely cuddly Sunday Muppets at home watching alpine skiing kinda chair, it's a blankey-chair, I wanted to turn this whole place into a chill-out pad with tables and those lights that shine a bar sorta thing straight up to the ceiling, and when smoke gets in it it looks amazing, but I don't smoke anymore, so I wouldn't know.

The mirror ball disappears into the ceiling, and he stows his sabre onto the side of the chair. He removes his hood.

For those who don't know me, I'm Richie Excellent, cuz I have a good time. The caterer, I know, he didn't show, so I apologize for there beinalackasatay; I know the guy too, he's a friend, but it's like, c'mon, "Nantha," or whatever he's called in his "homeland": "Malaysia," "Mexico," "Manitoba," "M" something; I'm rambling, I know, you get used to it, I'm against full stops... mostly. If you haven't partied with me, forgive my brain, I suffer from tangential warfare, I get off track. The ladies find it charming.

A camera FLASH goes off.

On the screen: "Thank you for coming." *And it's gone.*

I apologize for the must and the mildew, the mites, for the dampness of the hay, the chill of the night air, the blister on my thumb, the rhymes that are dumb, the fetid water, the bile, the flies, the farts. I meant to wash but... I got thinkin' and... you know how it goes. Peace.

He makes the peace sign.

Another camera FLASH goes off and he is blinded. He gets up, accusing:

Yo yo, what's with the flashcubes, ya hairy tourist. Tryin' to distract me? Your phone gonna ring as well? R-e-s-p-e-c-t, turn off your toys n don't fuck with me. You'll get your photo ops tomorrow, okay? Save it for tomorrow, Papa. Rotsy.

What? Are you scared, Richie? Of what? Go on. Get on with it.

Everything's changed so *rapidement* recently, so sudden, ya know, and sometimes it gets the better of you; you become all maudlin n stoic n all those great things when one chapter closes forever and another one stretches out to the horizon in front of you, you know what I'm sayin'? You get to a point in life that you know is a major turning point, and you make that turn, you flip that page, and you kinda know in the back of your mind where you're headed, but you can't really put it into words, can't finish the sentence, but know how it's gonna.... Like nostalgia for the future. And sometimes at that point, you get smacked with a huge sense of the common good, ya know? And ya realize that more than anything... you wanna make a change. A difference. Fer example, yer at brunch...

He returns to his throne to demonstrate.

...with the paper all spread out n really good coffee, n some stranger wants the sports section, n you don't care cuz you don't give a shit 'bout sports really, 'cept basketball, n so you say to the guy who wants the sports section: "Sure, man. Take it." And you contribute. You make a fuckin' difference—there I said it—and you make a difference in whatever way you can.

Well I'd gotten to such a point, man. I woke up one morning, looked out at the horizon in front of me, and I realized that I'd had it. Completely fucking had it. It was a time to make change and… I didn't have anything else to do that day… I was *(almost inhumanly drawn out)* reeeeeaaaallll-lyyyyyy… boooorrrrrreeddddd. *(and back to pace)* So… I sewed the Canadian flag onto my forehead, hopped on a plane, and booted it down to South America.

The screen shows pictures of a lush jungle landscape.

And man is that a place; totally recommend it: sand, surfing, awesome people, the *ladies*?! Damn! And right next to you is like actual rainforests, jungles like fuckin' Dagobah, man, pure perfection n soon to be devastated, logged n burned at the stake, sendin' animals runnin' for not only their lives but their souls, losin' their kids n leavin' their holes, and I see all this n I'm like, BANZAI: smacked with a path: I *know* it's a time to make change!

The jungle fades.

I'll look back on all this as a time to make change. If the National Film Board ever gets their hands on this story, they'll call it A *Time to Make Change*. I mean, there I was, Richie Excellent, not only *outside*, but like jungles n shit, get?! I mean, don't get me wrong, I don't "jog" or that shit.… I ain't one of those "I'm gonna check out BC for a bit" kinda guys.… I won't even buy drugs from yuppies. But I feel I have a responsibility. We all do. And sometimes trail mix is just trail mix.

He stands with his sabre.

And in my little spin around the rainforest, I heard rumour of this tribe causing some substantial damage to the rainforests; yeah, seriously, chopping and slashing for "homes." And there's me, pig-in-shit-fulla-hope thinking we've got to share this planet, work together! It doesn't do anybody any good to just sit around and wait for someone *else* to change the world, you gotta get out there, man, ya gotta *lead*: cuz someone else could really fuck it up, right? Damn right. I dug in. After some careful planning, I awoke one morning at the break of dawn, had myself a hearty breakfast, hired a handful of mercenaries, and I shot each and every member of that tribe while they prayed in a church we built them.

He smiles at us. Smug bastard. If this were a movie from the forties, another character who'd been watching him would say at this point... "Heeyy, what's his game?" He takes his sabre, dear friend and childhood icon, sweeps it up, and plants it before him like a Clockwork Orange *cane.*

(evangelical) My naaaaame's Richie Excellent cuz I have a good time; I'm the Slim Shady, baby: and this is my rhyme.

Music.

On screen: "TO ALL OF YOU," *which fades to black.*

And then "AND TO SUSIE," *and then below:* "WHO GAVE ME THE PILL."

Opening credits on screen, Blair-Witchy in their production quality, followed by a quote:

"How dares thy harsh rude tongue sound this unpleasing news?
What Eve, what serpent hath suggested thee
To make a second fall of cursed man?"

And then fade-in beneath: "—Shakespeare" *in that real old Shakespeare's-signature font.*

Meanwhile, during the credits… RICHIE *knights the audience. He tests out his sabre, thrusting and parrying, a mix of fencing and Jedi swordplay. He notices a fly buzzing around his head and goes after it, swiping here and there with the lightsabre until eventually abandoning the sabre and swatting at the fly with his hands. Once he notices the fly has landed on the TV, he goes for it with the sabre and embeds it in the TV, forced to abandon it there. He finally catches the fly in his hand and executes a little dance, shaking his fists about vigorously, before releasing the fly and watching as it buzzes around dizzily and eventually falls to the ground.* RICHIE *stamps the fucker.*

Screen out. Music out.

He notices the audience is still there—he'd been so caught up in lightsabre technique and dancing and fly chasing, he'd forgotten who he was, where he was, what he was; in short he had forgotten about the people. Who are now are staring at him. So he admits:

PART I

RICHIE Okay, I was never in South America. HEHEHEHEHEheheheh.

He thinks this is funnier than they.

I wish. It'd be seriously... different. It was... a cover. I left a message at my folks saying I was in South America, when really I was coming here, figuring they'd understand my need to screw off for a while. And this ain't my place, it's where I'm at, it's where I've been; if I was actually living here I'd groove it up a bit: a little shag is what I'm sayin', a little bamboo is what I'm sayin', a little somethin' Korean-Japanesy. But. I am visiting. And you are visiting me, Richie Excellent. The First. Um. I'm supposed to read this.

He reaches into his pocket and pulls out an envelope, opens it, clears his throat, and reads:

"Welcome Public. You have been selected randomly as a representative sampling of the population. The time has come to spill the beans, and we anxiously await the reactions and / or opinions expressed by you here today. They will offer those in charge of... *(RICHIE can't read it because it's been xxxed out)* something xxxed out, and below-mentioned sponsors, first and foremost "Sports team / Burger chain," an understanding of how the world will react when this is announced officially tomorrow at the gala. Return to what you were saying, Richie." Oh. So.

He folds up the paper and returns it to his pocket.

Apparently we don't want the earth stunned into a state of riot, or the markets to crash, or George W. to get wiggy n blame some Middle Eastern nation or something.... No, no we don't... no.... So, take the news and pass it on... but gently...

He is nervous.

I'm not entirely sure how you're gonna take this. I mean, I rehearsed this over and over again in my mind, but now that you're here... n bein so nice... I don't know how to do this. It seems my folks eventually got concerned, n my mom probaly panicked, n then probaly wasn't long before word got out I was *dead*...

On S2 is a sequence of quotes:

"Uneducated Youth Goes Missing"
—*Toronto Star*

"Poor Economy Causes Youth's Disappearance"
—*National Post*

"New-fangled Drug 'Ecstasy' Claims Yet Another"
—*Globe and Mail*

"Duh. Kid Go Bye Bye in Scawee Jungle"
—*Toronto Sun*

...so I'm sorry if I've caused you stress n undue duress. I'm afraid the press went to town with my "disappearance." I almost backed out. I almost didn't sign the paper, I almost wasn't here today. What would I tell people? What would I say? "No, Miss Reporter, I'm actually fine"?! Just march right outta here and make up some—

WHAM: another camera FLASH. RICHIE is interrupted by the appearance of CANDI Phurburger (pronounced "fur-BUR-ger") on screen. She is on location outside a building: grey, stone, pillars, Osgoode-ish. Monotoned

Sounds Like She's Bored Out of Her Skull Reporter But She's Actually At the Top of Her Game What's With All the Capitals:

CANDI We are here live, awaiting the release of young, determined Richie Excellent, be*lieved* to have *fal*len into a volcano while *tra*velling in South A*me*rica some month and a half ago. While he acknowledges scars from "branches" and what are being called "bug bites," he denies reports of his death, saying, quote: "Give me a break, I mean I'm right here in front of you, what's up with that? C'mon, nah, wasn't me, man, no, it wasn't. Quit with the dumbass questions, you nosy, monotoned Dilbert-reading-mouth-breather, asking everyone else questions for a living will not absolve you of your need to feel involved. Fuck you." End quote.

On screen we see RICHIE leaving the building behind her. CANDI and cameraman rush over to get a question in, and on the way, CANDI trips and falls, making some gurgle noise as she disappears from sight. A beat of nothing and then she's up again, running over to meet RICHIE.

How do you feel, Mr. Excellent?

SCREEN RICHIE

Whoa! What's up with your face?

The camera pans over to CANDI, who has a bloody nose and bashed forehead from falling. She smiles at the camera. And slogs on:

CANDI How does it feel to be alive?

SCREEN RICHIE

Pretty much the same, Candi.

CANDI We understand you were chased by natives with poison-tipped blow darts.

And he looks at her. Better than her.

SCREEN RICHIE

That's right, Candi, I ran and I ran. And when I got to the river, I shouted to my friend in the boat plane to "Start the engine! Start the engine!" but he couldn't hear me cuz he was fishing, so I guess it was just plain ol' luck that there happened to be a vine hanging there that I could use to swing myself into the water. It was an adventure. When I finally got into the plane there was a snake in there with me. I hate snakes, Candi, I hate 'em. Hey, whatchu doin' later, anyway?

The screen fades to black. On stage:

RICHIE But that didn't happen at all. I didn't back outta nuthin'. I'm the real deal. Anyways,

He notices the movement of his arm, enjoying the fact that…

I'm alive.

Pause.

N they've treated me real good here too. Pure, unadulterated, hot towel, royal treatment: they even offered me whores, can you believe it?! And just to show them how indifferent I am about absolutely everything, cuz that's the nature of Richie Excellent, I responded to the offer of whores with *(long beat)* "BOO-YAH!" Which was cool. Anything I wanted to make my stay more enjoyable, they said. Booze, pills, coke "up to my ears," all of which I declined. I swore to myself to keep this body a temple for the big day, and besides, there were a coupla unretrievable years with coke a ways back… I think…

Pause.

But I'm not here to talk about drugs… or sex… this is *awesome*! It's like… *live* or something… it's nice… like—

And then the words rush out of RICHIE *so fast and furious that it's all he can do to keep up with them:*

—goin' out to yer favourite place n getting there early n feeling like a big dink cuz no one wanted to go out until later or maybe not at all but you just had to get out there and you end up meeting some excellent people who don't want to fuck you or fight you and you end up having a hoot with these great new people who you care about a lot. And ya laugh at it all, at the whole fucked up way the world works n think it's all pretty amazing when it comes down to it on the long walk home through Kensingston Market as the dew breaks. And that truck is there with the cages fulla chickens that can't move there's so many of them in there and it's pretty much the most harsh existence you can imagine yet somehow hugely metaphorical, it's a moment of too much when I say, "Too much moment, man," you feel overloaded with data, being given too much all at once, shoved at you like dinner you can't ever finish you're full, you're full but there's more, there's more, and the more you get the less you can put it all together and it's only gonna get worse cuz the show's just begun but if you could just get a single breath… in there somewhere… it would be okay. *(He gets a breath, slows down.)* It would all be okay. A second or two away from the information buffet packed with MSG that makes us drowsy, but damn, it's yummy… tastes like chicken. Information tastes like cages full of chickens… in Kensington Market… on the long walk home… *(And then speeds up again.)* This is harsh so you quickly think of friendly things like *Miami Vice* or Polaroid film or *Canadian* fuckin' *Idol* because cultural lint: it salves the soul. Or you think of that once in a blue moon when a crossword is the best, taking it to brunch, paper all spread out, stranger about to receive the sports section with courtesy. Comfort like the smell of dry cleaning…. Comfort like the smell of dry humping… a hug from a dear friend… this, right now, feels like one of those times, and I know I'm avoiding telling you what you're here to find out… but I'm a little freaked out, dudes. Freaked like of the uncle who pulls quarters out of his ears and thinks it's amazing but sorta lingers after, smilinatcha. 'K. Well firstly, I didn't mean for this to happen! It was an accident, I swear. I sorta… stumbled onto destiny. Birthed by Must See TV.

We hear the sound of a newborn baby's cry: "WAH!" Richie takes the throne, at home, kickin' back with the TV Guide.

It all started at my place. My real place. I'm there markering up the new guide for the coming week's viewing: green for must-see, red: stay-away. And this special catches my attention called *Charting the Genome*: brainy, very dense, very today. CBC without wagons: it'll be decent. So I give it a yellow or amber marking. And it was slotted right between *Degrassi: The Next Generation* and *Train 48*: whatchugonnado, that's like the big night, right? And I'd already been watching for like five hours; I was all stiff and not about to "stand," so I end up watching it… and this guy…

On screen we see footage of GENE *as a car salesman type, cowboy hat, waving people to "come on down" or some such, standing in front of somewhere with those li'l plastic flags and a blinking phone number at the bottom of the screen.*

…this scientist guy who's like a cross between that dude from *Third Rock* and Dr. Zed from *Owl* magazine comes on and starts goin' off like some ol' car salesman about how he is looking for people in the coveted 18–35 year old demographic to participate in a study: big bucks, no experience necessary, that he would "gladly entertain interested parties," is what he said.

Next thing I know, I'm an "interested party." Fuckin' right I'm an "interested party," I mean whatcha got?! I'm the Jerry's kid of the attention-deficit-experience-hungry, you know what I'm sayin? I'm *thee* interested party. I couldn't leave *that* alone, I couldn't *not* do it. I mean, do you eat the cereal and then chuck the prize out with the. bathwater... or something? No. No you don't. I'm so pumped I don't even phone to check this out. I just land. At his office... this place... that's like *(searching)* Ikea-chrome-Christina-Ricci-*Dead-Ringers*-green-apple... and I'm there *without* an appointment. I'm wild, n I just march my butt right in there and I wait my turn like a good ol' Canuck. I don't wanna be a bother to anyone. I want to follow the rules. I want to do what I am supposed to do, *what am I saying—*

> *The camera FLASH goes off, again blinding RICHIE. He searches again for its source and accuses:*

Don't! Okay?! Fuck. Look, I don't know who you are or where you're sitting, but that's pretty bright... and there are no sunglasses on this Excellent face. Do you see sunglasses? Do you see sunglasses? No. No you don't. *Pas de* sunglass. It throws me off my train... choo choo... what was I... what was I thinking...

> *On screen we see a picture of a Big Mac.*

No.

> *And then a famine-stricken child.*

Peh.

And then a blossoming flower.

No.

And then Carrie Fisher as Princess Leia in that sexy Return of the Jedi *gold bikini.*

No.

Then a shot of a glowstick hitting the pavement.

Right.

The screen goes out.

(back to business) So I'm sitting in the waiting room, tearing through the latest copy of *Vice* magazine to discover what the people at Gypsy Co-op will be wearing next month, when suddenly it's my turn, I'm called in, and I'm sitting across the table from the old guy from the commercial. It's like meeting a star. So I take a moment and say to myself as I do so many days of my life, "You're okay, Richie, you're already in the haunted house: just hold tight and learn to ride: riding it defeats the fear." So I transfer my Fear into my Determination pile: single click and drag.

I couldn't believe I'd gotten this far, that this guy's giving me the time of goshdarn day, I mean, don't they see who they're taking seriously here? They *must.* He takes my name, address, the basics, and then goes on to family history, illness, tattoos, and scars, and then he asks me if I have any *hobbies…* like stamp collecting for example…

Music: awful, scraping-the-bottom-of-the-barrel club music, such as one would find on a Top 10 HMV compilation or some such shite: muscle-car techno.

Be brave, Richie. Be kind. Let them know what they're dealing with here. Confess: that "No, I don't collect stamps, mister..."

On screen: glowsticks flying through space. Light show. Disco ball.

"...I watch *Electric Circus,* baby. I'm a fan... of *Electric Circus,*" I tell him. "Tapes of it," I tell him. "My tapes are dewey-decimaled and documented by date, guest artist, and which of the beautiful and talented *EC* dancers are featured most that particular week. *(moving his arms, "voguing" like an* Electric Circus *dancer)* I watch *Electric Circus* to know I'm alive, mister. Because as long as those people are doing... *that* to their personalities... then I'm allowed to consider myself *above* them. And I need that. We all wanna feel better than something. That's why we keep the homeless around. That's why we've canonized the Osbornes. That's why we watch *Jerry Springer* and his circus-sideshow-retarded-lesbian-three-legged-midget-reincarnated-makin'-a-difference-in-their-community-trailer-trash-goth-boys discussin' the topic: "What I Love To Fuck and Kill." So that finally there is someone who is worse off." I told him all this.

"Gene," as I would come to know him, leans back, obviously interested, intrigued, enchanted even, and he looks at me real close, dead in the eyes, and says like some old cowboy: "Kid... let's get breakfast." *(beat)* This is just a bit odd, but I don't argue: go with the flow, Richie, go with the flow. I talk when I'm nervous. as you now know: I. can't. go. slow. So I just kept babbling, relentless, comin' down like a monsoon, knock you out, momma said knock you out.

The music and screen cut out.

"My favourite *EC* must have been 12/07/02." For those who don't remember, that was the one where Laneej wore the *orange* cowboy hat and Jamie shaved his armpits. Now are you with me people? Come on. Let's see those hands! Raise it! Raise it! 'Member? And there were those three classic acned girls in from Mississauga standing outside with the sign begging to see Rick the Temp's bum? 'Member ? *(long beat)* Me neither really. I taped over it by accident. I panicked, needing a tape for the premiere of *Survivor: Pearl Islands*: I mean that crazy Rupert even looks like a pirate. Anyways, fuck. What's done is done. We move forwards.

Though if you're ever up for it, watch eight hours or so straight of alternating *Electric Circus* and *Survivor*: your brain starts functioning at such a low frequency it is guaranteed to fuck you up, man. Once I started to think that one of the beautiful and talented *EC* dancers was gonna get booted out of the building, I was tired... but I felt for the dancer who was gonna get Survivored off Znaimer's Island... on some cold and blowy night in the winter, I mean, can you imagine? Some post-pubescent Tammy Faye with a name like Shaleece. or Rhona. or Fondle. or Clorette. or Cathy. or Jenny. or something-ee.

like Cherry. or "Zowie," the ultimate in "alternative" rich-kids names, or Nancy-Fancy-Snatch or Nebuchadnezzar or whatever, man, head to toe in sparkles and sequins standing outside the Starbucks, crying into her non-fat soy mochallukkachuckafuckinchino... and she takes her twelve-dollar glowstick that she bought to make her feel a part of the "innovative" rave crowd and lets it slip from her hand to the earth...

On screen we see the glowstick leaving the girl's hand and hitting the pavement. On stage, RICHIE mimics the fall of the glowstick: a leaf falling from a tree.

... and she blames her lot in life on Rob Brezsny and his insightful, well-meaning horoscope and the ample-breasted Laneej, who she knows will always be prettier than her, and she screams, screams up at the heavens, streaky-cheeked and latte-lipped: because the experience before her consists of the universe crumbling around her. Pity is not a great characteristic for a leader. I know. But the more I consider... the more something feels. familiar.

He takes his throne, thoughtful.

And some things are just plain ol' sad. Like the fact that the only art form left to us... *(pointing to himself)* is irony. I don't think deep down I am a cynic. I mean, I wanna lose my voice with cheering but I find it hard to see... and I know I continue to avoid the point of it all, but somehow this all relates: trust the thread. It's like... sometimes I feel... like a locomotive burning up its steam... or a Warner Brothers minivan fulla gasoline...

He follows this rhyme.

Flyin' down the highway lookin kinda mean,
eyes bugged out cuz I'm high on caffeine.
Pull into the drive-through, don't make a scene:
"Gimme an extra-large coffee, hold the sugar and—"

RICHIE is interrupted by a FLASH and the appearance of GENE on screen, little bit of icing stuck near his mouth, who completes RICHIE's rhyme with:

GENE Cream?

And then we see RICHIE and GENE sitting at a table in a food court, having breakfast…

SCREEN RICHIE
No. So. This is big, dude.

GENE It's the biggest.

SCREEN RICHIE
Yeah.

GENE Amaretto?

SCREEN RICHIE
What what?

GENE Is the icing amaretto?

SCREEN RICHIE
Okay, you're skeevin' me out, dude. This whole thing is like, skeevy.

GENE puts the Danish down, cuts into it.

GENE Look, kid. You can judge me all you want, but when you come right to it, there ain't no more right or wrong, there's no more morality: we're past it, it don't apply. So if I were you, I'd spend less time judging the "sitch," and more time accepting it.

SCREEN RICHIE
(sounding out a new word) "Mo-ral-i-ty"?

GENE There's no choice here, it's happening: we move forward, kid, that's what we do. The slate is clean; the question is: are you gonna be the chalk.

GENE, misplacing his gruntles, is thus disgruntled.

SCREEN RICHIE
You got a motorhome?

GENE And a real nice watch.

SCREEN RICHIE
Would I get a motorhome?

GENE You'd get anything you want, anything, but if you tell anyone about this till we tell you to, *if* we tell you to, and BAF.

Pause.

SCREEN RICHIE
Whatju tell *your* peeps?

GENE "Peeps"?

SCREEN RICHIE
Uhh… how you say, uh: "friends, family, those you are… representing."

GENE (*nervous*) Nah, never saw the point of it, no, no, never wanted a family, expensive, noisy, my work… growing old in the same bed, flaked skin, I like to have my things where I know I can find them.

SCREEN RICHIE
Really? You never wanted—

GENE No, I never wanted a family, now quit talking back.

SCREEN RICHIE
Sorry, I'm just asking. (*pause*) I wanna do good things. I wanna help.

GENE You are the worst option available.

SCREEN RICHIE
Aw c'mon, it'd be fuckin' wicked, man.

GENE Would it.

SCREEN RICHIE
Yeah, it'd be fuckin' excellent.

GENE Excellent, eh?

SCREEN RICHIE
What the hell else am I gonna do, hunh? Look at me. Make this *me*.

GENE picks up RICHIE's application form.

GENE Moved away from home after dropping out of school, spends time smoking pot, listening to "house" music, and the occasional surf. Last book read: *Dick and Jane*, have you even *heard* of Shakespeare?!

SCREEN RICHIE
Help me Obi-Wan Kenobi, you're my only hope. *(looping)* Help me Obi-Wan Kenobi, you're my only hope / Help me Obi-Wan Kenobi, you're my only hope.

We hear the loop of the above continuing as we get a shot of GENE watching this kid, almost in disbelief and oddly fascinated.

GENE You bein' funny ?

SCREEN RICHIE
Yeah, I'm bein' funny, and if you don't like it you can laugh about *this*, old man.

RICHIE whips out a lightsabre and swings it across the table to cut GENE down. We then see GENE's clothes fall, like Ben Kenobi being cut down by Darth Vader.

Cut to RICHIE at the table, shaking off this daydream.

GENE You bein' funny?

SCREEN RICHIE
Yeah.

GENE Hunh.

GENE realizes how ridiculously deliciously ironically perfect a choice RICHIE would be, recognizing himself as a younger man, studying himself as a younger man. The decision made, GENE gathers papers into his briefcase, etc.

Drop by the office Monday to draw up a contract. I'll need signatures of release on a number of forms. There may be pain involved, there may not be; it's hard to tell... with pain. Leave blood and urine when you drop off the forms. Monday for signatures, Tuesday we get jiggy.

SCREEN RICHIE *wipes the bit of icing off of* GENE's *face. Then as* GENE *is leaving, one last warning:*

And remember: I tell you when to spill the beans.

RICHIE nods as GENE is gone. Then a slow zoom in on RICHIE's face, dreamy, imagining all that will be his when he is king.... Screen out.

Spot up on RICHIE, nervous, about to come clean. Spill the beans, boy. He takes a long time and then finally, it comes out:

RICHIE I... *cloned* myself, man. I fuckin' *cloned* myself. I mean... why not, right? Why the fuck not?!

He puts a hand to his mouth and bites a nail.

The screen comes on to show the hosts of an Entertainment Tonight*-type show. Behind them we see stars, red carpets, some huge Hollywood event. Our stereotypes:*

BUD Hi everyone, I'm Bud Chest.

BEIGE *Et je suis* Beige, here awaiting the arrival of Richie Excellent and "friend," isn't that wonderful ?

BUD Oh, it's wonderful, Beige, absolutely everyone's here: Drew, Mandela, Penny Marshall, Charlton Heston, and Pat Buchanan have arrived *together*—

BEIGE Oh, finally.

BUD Alice Cooper'll be singing "School's Out," I'm not exactly sure why though…

They laugh. Yuk yuk. The film fades to black.

On stage, RICHIE stands, arms outstretched, holding the lightsabre and triumphant, ruler over us all.

RICHIE I… am… the most major historical figure of the new millenium.

And he goes to his throne, the smug portrait of the king.

There are bodyguards amongst you, so get thee ready for a strip search equal to nothin' no A-rab's felt in the last little while: tight. You see true believers, the entire planet is gonna go nuts wantin' a piece o' me: tours, signings, conventions, leading to trading cards, action figures, Saturday-morning cartoon, leading to biopic, clothing line, McRichie Meal, all leading up to *two* lifetime achievement awards. Planet Hollywood is booked for the announcement party. Mike Bullard is hosting because he's funny, talented, and deserving. I've invited Sean Desmond cuz I thought it'd be funny to watch no one hang out with him. And I've left specific instructions as regards Ben Mulroney. Send him an invite but don't let him in… and we'll all hide n watch him outside dribblin' cum outta his mouth he's trying so hard to get in. The promoters have gone so far as to exhume the body of Bill Maher for use as pinata… while Dennis Miller and Michael Moore, the surviving of the furies, cower in the corner and weep. While I, somewhere safe n hopeful, am muttering "It'll be okay. It'll be okay." Because if what we called "murderers" became what we called "warriors" became what we called "soldiers" became what we called "peacekeepers" became what we now call "heroes," I figure *my* stakes at herodom are better than even odds.

The mirror ball descends to his hand.

I hold up the mirror… to see the world… and the bravest part of me declares: how *funny.* HAHAHAHAHAHA.

BOOM: music in as RICHIE spins in the throne.

MONTAGE

During which our onstage RICHIE does some simple dance sequence, which eventually breaks down as the montage nears its end…

The screen cuts back to BUD and BEIGE wrapping up their segment:

BUD So welcome one and all to the surprise "Gala to Open the Doors to the Next Age of Man Brought to You by the Sony Playstation 2."

Cut to a STONED GUY, probably an old friend of RICHIE's who shall enjoy shop class well into his thirties.

STONED GUY I don't say this about everyone… but if Elvis were alive, he'd be Richie Excellent.

Cut to some homies on the street:

HOMIES RICHIE'S THE BEST, etc.

Cut to RICHIE throwing money into the air.

Cut to three girls in Speaker's Corner talking about their idol:

GIRLS Oh he's so awesome, I really love him, like, I've got all these posters… etc.

Cut to RICHIE and his brand-new motorhome.

Cut to a talk-show host talking to two RICHIES.

HOST So, movie deals, *Just the Two of Us* an international bestseller, and now I understand, a recording contract. Is there anything left for you two to accomplish?!

Cut to a British Peter-Ustinov-royal-biographer-type-but-a-woman taking a delightful look back at RICHIE's rise:

BROADCASTER
The initial meeting between Richie Excellent and Queen Elizabeth went off without a hitch. The two were apparently twittering like old school chums about Richie's request for not only a castle, but a village, *and* a knighthood for *Star Wars* creator, George Lucas.

Cut to a series of photos:

RICHIE with George W.

RICHIE with the pope.

RICHIE arriving somewhere with Paris Hilton.

RICHIE hanging with Michael Jackson: he's been diddled.

Cut to RICHIE giving a speech.

SCREEN RICHIE
I don't like bombs much… um. The cheap cheeseburger day at McDonald's is really good; I'm *for* that.

Cut to RICHIE with a brand-new Nike swoosh tattoo on his foot.

Cut to a minister.

MINISTER This *is* the Second Coming.

Cut to a coupla' dykey-lookin' protestors holding placards reading "Stop Cloning Now" and "Stop Abortion Now."

PROTESTOR 1 We don't want life given—

PROTESTOR 2 —and we don't want it taken away.

We cut to a couple on a couch, the man is pregnant.

WIFE We wanted his eyes—

HUSBAND But her sense of humour.

They laugh.

Cut to some kid spray-painting something in an alley.

Cut to two little kids throwing "Richios" cereal everywhere.

Cut to the guy finishing his spray-painting: an "R2" tag.

Cut back to RICHIE, again at the podium, concluding his speech:

SCREEN RICHIE
And say it with me: free at last, free at last…

He steps aside. His clone steps in…

Thank God Almighty we are free at last.

Cut to RICHIE, speaking directly to camera.

And they told two friends. *(The image doubles like the Head and Shoulders commercial of old.)* And they told two friends. *(It doubles again.)* And so on. *(And again.)* And so on.

The screen image dissolves into a cell dividing, as through a microscope.

This dissolves into a small group of people, like a city sidewalk at noon or something.

And then into a larger group of people.

And an even larger group… like a nation's worth of people.

And then into a picture of the earth as from space.

And finally stars.

Le Fin du Montage.

On stage, RICHIE is bothered. Something inside him is… uncomfortable.

The stage goes black.

"INTERMISSION"

On screen, still stars, but fading in on top is the word "EXHALE." We hear cold arctic wind. "EXHALE" fades out and is replaced by "INHALE" because it's now time for:

PART II

Lights up on RICHIE, staring off into the night.

RICHIE

A long time ago, in a galaxy far far away, there lived a young man who realized his destiny was to embarrass the world.

RICHIE, please, don't get heavy on us, brother.

Right. It's good to get that off my chest. That there's two of me now. The first. And second. And it's odd, it's weird, cuz, I mean, I'm pretty good at repressin' stuff, like I thought I'd just file this snuggly next to my racism and potential cancer files but… something is… sorry, I'm cool. It's all good. It's all good.

RICHIE. Come on.

It's just… I find myself… "*caring*," and I know I said to Gene, "I wanna do good things," you know, pullin' out my generation's stock skill of whippin' into the psychic phone booth n changin' from jaded cynic to Zen master in two point five: "I want world peace—if I got time." But I'm *believin'* it! And I'm indifferent, dammit, that's the nature of Richie Excellent…. Why am I talking to you like this, fuckin' corn dog, man, it's supposed to be a good time, and there I go once again totally pointing out an already obvious character flaw, fuck man, I am so metaphorical sometimes, I mean, why not just take a picture it'll last longer.

FLASH! He is suddenly strangely focused.

I remember. My hand burning. Chompin' on a Pop-Tart that's too hot n escaping out back n sitting on the stairs n starin' up at… staaarrrs… n wondering what it'd be like without anybody around. Without any humans. Which is weird now, cuz now I've cloned myself and that's sorta thee… opposite. of nobody around. It'd be lonely. Boring. There'd be nowhere to go on the weekend. Greeeen.

On screen: pairs of animals: elephants, monkeys, birds, lab rabbits…

And all the animals just go about their bouncy animal lives fulla makin' love n hanging out in trees n shit and… and…

Where ya goin', buddy?

…and the seals don't get clubbed for Mrs. Allenhoffer's twentieth wedding anniversary present. A fur coat. From her husband. Who actually wants her dead cuz he's having fabulous porno sex with Miss Poole, who lives only a few doors down and coincidentally owns a pool.

Then on screen is footage from some tacky daytime soap. RICHIE is remembering something.

And she invites him over to her peanut-shaped pool for iced tea and he hangs up and says: "I'm just going for a walk," and Mrs. Allenhoffer says "All right," and grits her teeth: "My, he's gone for a lot of walks lately," and she watches the TV and gets so sad inside, cuz it makes her feel even worse, and she knows this, but feels she deserves it.

Screen fades to black. RICHIE more intense.

And when he gets back from his quick screw in the pool with Poole, he presents his wife with a fur coat. "It smells pretty," she says. It smells pretty because Miss Poole didn't want it anymore and Mr. Allenhoffer thought it would be the perfect gift for his wonderful wife on the event of their twentieth year of being ever so happily married in wedded bliss. THAT, fer instance, would not have happened if we weren't around, right? If we weren't around, there'd just be a seal on the ice somewhere, sittin' with his pals, and thinking 'bout fish I guess.

On screen: a harp seal.

I haven't thought about that in. forever. Strange what life makes you.

On screen the seal turns into hearts flying through space.

Music out. Screens out. The mood lingers, though RICHIE tries to cover it.

That Gene guy man, I uh… I felt sorry for him… next thing ya know I'm wiping his mouth cuz there was a bit a food that he wouldn't have known was there. Amaretto. Icing. That he woulda walked away with, as old guys tend to do, and be one of those dudes you see with the bit of food on his face and you think, "Fuck, I'm gonna look away NOW cuz that's not really happening, and I am

NEVer gonna be like that," 'cept I'm actually gonna be much worse cuz the drugs are harder now. Although technically I won't really "age" at all—I mean they're planning to build "me's" at age two, twenty, forty, sixty, eighty. I'll be able to sit with an old Richie and listen to what my life was like when I was my age. But right here, n right now, I feel like I'm Yoda and I'm *four hundred* years old n I'm dyin', here today deliverin' my final message before I go hang with Obi-Wan down by Craft Services or the Blue Screen er whatever, an' I'm askin' you to draw near and list when I say: *(imitating Yoda)* There is… another… Skywalker. *(back to RICHIE)* And I don't know how to explain this to him.

A bigger FLASH than we're used to goes off, throwing RICHIE literally off balance. He stands.

All right, look, buddy, c'mon man, fuck, look, I've asked you nicely. I don't want to have to ask you again.

RICHIE's voice changes… he is channelling his mother.

(as Mom) Don't make me come in there. Open this door immediately. Richie? Richie? Can I come in? I'm coming in.

The screen shows the arctic vista again. RICHIE is trying to shake off this memory.

We hear the Final Jeopardy music, a little "off," a little wobbly.

(as Mom) I made some oatmeal-orange cookies, Richie, are you hungry? Sandwich? Stir-fry? Sushi? Corn? Lamb, would you like some lamb? Heroin? Salt? Sand? What were you doing? *(as himself)* I-I-I-I-I I was watching some TV. *(as Mom)* Well do your own darn dishes, boy-o. *(as himself)* Look, I'm sorry Dad's screwing the hot neighbour, 'aight?!

The Jeopardy *music completes with a ding: time's up, let's check your answers, and is gone.*

(as Mom) I'll be in the kitchen.

We hear a phrase of the theme music from Coronation Street *as RICHIE's headache leaves him..*

And then she took away my television!

RICHIE rushes to his beloved TV.

She explained it was making me "strange," preventing me from developing "social skills necessary for passage into adulthood." I think she just needed to take something from someone. And that's fine... but... it's *TV* and... not having... the television being taken away twisted me up sumpin' awful inside, I mean, what's a kid to do, *read a book*?!

Fine, granted, it's all Dini-fucking-petty, get over it, blah de fuckin' blah, but the world turned... incomprehensible. Like that ejected *Electric Circus* girl standing there with her hands emptying of a crumbled universe, nothing made sense anymore! I felt stupid! And I wanna be taken serious! *Joshua Tree* serious. I'm tellin' ya, the new celebrity is gonna be genetic pioneers, and if that's the case I'm like grade seven Canadian history I'm such a pioneer. I'm already scheduled for a star on the Canadian Walk of Fame; can you imagine anything more lucrative? I'll be downloaded! I'm so hard a testicle has been engulfed by my shaft. I could give my girl *two* Richies; wonder if she could handle it. HARHARHAR… eh heh heh. *(Now I got an idea, more and more manic.)* I'll fuck mahself! Like that wouldn't mess you up a bit. I mean really *fuck* myself. I'll practise my breathing and I'll treat me right. Finally someone who knows what I like. *What if only one of us is into it??*

On screen we are travelling down the hallway of a house towards the front door, then out and down to the end of the walk where a TV sits.

Right. So the TV goes out on a Friday and sits at the end of the walk forever… a discarded jack-o'-lantern turning in on itself like an apple doll, a shrunken head posted to warn of danger, a great suburban paperweight plunked there, keeping our house from flying away in the wind. And me, staring at it, realizing my life, every sentence outta my mouth, comes from that box, and there it sits, all my analogy, all points of reference, clinging to the earth. Life without TV: people have done it.

The camera circles the TV set again and again.

Come Sunday my dad gets that weird dad angst about the fur coat he'd given my mom, and he snaps, slams open the door and goes to the end of the walk, towards It, I assumed to bring It back, some valiant dad effort to save his kid from suicidal boredom what's going on…

On screen a brief image of Hal from 2001. *Watching us. And gone.*

Don't touch it! Don't touch the fucking TV! Leave it! Cuz everybody'll be in trouble if you lift up that TV. Kingdoms will fall! If you lift that up it will set in motion events that.... My dad went to the end of the walk, picked up the TV, and took it over to Miss Poole's basement den. A gift. Felt like he had to give *her* something after the fur coat thing. Bein' fair, I guess. There since day one, nursing, soothing, a show for every mood, a station for every hour, and now you've taken my parent and given it to a *whore*!

And then the harshest FLASH of light and blast of noise yet: a mixture of band saws, scratching, and lightsabres clashing. RICHIE *stumbles and falls to the ground.*

Silence. He tries to get up.

And then the blast again, and RICHIE *is flattened, wounded, exhausted, it's flooding back now.*

Soon after I got quiet n I waited. I'd had it! Completely fucking had it. I needed a sign. Sitting on the ice, waiting for a sign. And meeting this lonely old scientist dude, something... recognized itself... oh man... my head is achin'... quakin'... Buster Brownie bakin'.

Life's flashing before me in digital THX.

60 frames a second.

150 beats a minute.

Dolby. stereo. sound.

I was born with a silver spoon. stuck. between the Baby Gap in my teeth.

He realizes he is rapping… and lets the memories wash over…

And then a week, a month, a year goes by, and I'm five,
and Kiss comes *Alive!* in first grade lemonade
rain on my parade, I didn't mean to hurt that
kid with my lightsabre toy,
man I got in trouble and it really burst my bubble,
almost blinded him…
but he's got his Orange Crush, he'll be okay.

On stage, RICHIE turns to an imaginary collection of records and selects one, taking it out of its sleeve and putting it on the imaginary turntable. He puts imaginary headphones on and drops an imaginary needle on the imaginary record—music—and RICHIE gets busy. Totally. Not. Imaginary.

Through the rap, the screen flips through product logos.

Crying when my dog it died,
I check beneath the bed he's dead with his head
resting on a stick of Juicy Fruit. gum.
Yum yum. rub a dub dub
"double your pleasure" embedded on my brain
forever,
never never keep my teeth from the grind, act
like I don't mind

and don't feel a thing, the audience is listening.
And shifting: is this real or pretend?
Unsure of what you're seeing?
Come see the show again.
Cuz I'm blastin off, I'm breakin' down borders,
Actin' all like that Harrison Forder,
or Columbus or… "Flagellan"?
Something like that I don't 'member, how you
  spell it?
Plain and simple: I'm an explorer:
goin' down the river to "the horror, the horror."
Now. Let's get sumpin' straight:
I ain't your pal, yer friend, I'm just the latest
  funky trend
follow me I'll take you round the bend to shop at
Presto, sweatshops, torture n pesto, mmm mmm mmm,
  I'm a
Time bomb tickin' n talking n mockin'
n most of all rockin', how we're all just cogs turnin'
n I'm yearnin' to know before we blow: "Why
  can't we all just join Downward Dog?" Um. No.
I am your high-speed connection,
Your T-dot conception of a techno erection,
and when I build it, you. will. cum. AAH! Then I
roll over n leave ya, wouldn't wanna be ya,
lean back my head to sleep, I'm lethal, Rip Van
Diesel against my family tree cuz I feel
so empty without mp.me
and another me, Google searchin' for dream, man,
but File not found cuz I'm a *telegram*!
Sayin' "Stop."
Hold it right there
State your case
Then get outta my face. So.
Two hundred years ago,
Europe imports the potato
in ships returned from far-off shores,

exciting and new, come aboard,
we're expecting you, to start farming, planting,
all the voices chanting:
"Faster n faster n bigger n better,
Grow that spud bigger n better."
They breed and feed
and they speed the breed, which impedes the seed.
Till. Boom. Bam: genetic strain
sends us off the rails on the crazy train
then lordy lordy it's 1840
Ireland's in the dopest famine
that's the crux of this groove I am in
trouble, trouble, pop-a-matic style,
nothin' grows no more and it takes a little while
but millions die and it's like a blueprint,
a bad aftertaste without the breath mint
or

The music cuts out.

floss.
Cuz of a lack of diversity.
UGH! HAH! History repeats itself so.
Sometimes you wanna go
back to the future, to paint the picture.
of. when. I. was

The music comes back in.

holidaying with Shelley Long
god knows she needs the work even if it's on
a Via train with Grimace, that McDonald's thing,
don't step to me brother, I'm the Burger King.
Tomb Raider
Lara Croft hands me a beer
and she welcomes me to my Carlsberg years,

The beat goes out of time.

I'm feelin' kinda dizzy
and brought to you by Disney
soundtracked by Moby,
pixellated babies…

The beat gets back in time.

Check my CV
pvcdvd. M.C. 3PO in my SUV KFC NBC ABC
Rick D, yo man, where's my E? F GBH I
can't think anymore I'm so fulla
CBSBSBSBSBSBSBSBS
all I got's my clenched fist
only weapon a phrase
a cliché, from the day:

Music out.

"I'll house you."

On screen we are circling the television at the end of the walk as earlier.

Churning the volumes of logos and slogans,
designs and catchphrases,
commercials and crazes.
I search through my past and conclude in my prattle:
we don't change a damn thing, we just add more channels!

On screen the television morphs into a gravestone.

My soul endorses a Microsoft Heaven, remote-controlled to subscribe to a Life Channel where everyone under the General Electric sun is a Tom Hanks martyr who must die on the cross and somewhere, a little little grave shall one day read "Richie Excellent TM."

Screen out. RICHIE is weak, sweating, out of breath. He cowers in his throne.

It'll be okay. It'll be okay.

FLASH! RICHIE spins around to face the screen.

Gene? Gene! I'm scared. I don't wanna go through with it. Gene?

GENE appears on screen, staring down at RICHIE on stage. He wears surgical gloves, his voice calm and hypnotic. We hear the pings of a heart monitor.

GENE *(screen)* Can you hear me all right?

RICHIE *(stage)* Yes, Gene.

GENE Are you afraid of needles, Richie?

RICHIE Well, they're *needles*, Gene.

GENE Are you a Darwinian?

RICHIE Hunh?

GENE Organ donor?

RICHIE I don't know.

GENE Plans of marriage, children, family, divorce? Plans of death? Plans of any kind? Sushi? Corn? Lamb, would you like some lamb? You're very lucky, you know.

RICHIE To be the first?

GENE Oh lord, you're not the first, you're… the star. You're going public.

RICHIE I've been reconsidering.

GENE We can erase that. Breathe.

RICHIE But what about the potato? Gene. Why are you doing this?

GENE tries to hide that he feels sorry for RICHIE… and so with some tenderness…

GENE Breathe.

GENE raises his hands into the shot and then zaps RICHIE, like the Emperor from Star Wars *zapping Luke, or the Wicked Witch of the West zapping the slippers on Dorothy's feet. The zapping complete, the screen fades to black.*

On stage, RICHIE does not move. It is silent for the first time in the show. No talking, no noise. It's beautiful. To have that again. Is he dead?

But then a sound… a single note… hardly audible at first and then getting louder. RICHIE's hand moves… he's alive. As the note crescendos, we see on screen the lush, beautiful jungle landscape as seen earlier. Then we watch as it turns into icy arctic tundra, and finally fades out.

RICHIE turns back to us.

RICHIE And Gene looked at me all caring n defeated n says, "I have to do this; it is my destiny: we move forwards, that's what we do. The apple waits to be plucked." And then he gives me a hug… and he looks me dead in the eye and says… he says: *(with accompanying gesture)* "Richie, in other words—"

He stops. Revolves around a full circle. And repeats words and gesture:

"In other words—"

He revolves another circle and repeats again:

"In other words—"

RICHIE is skipping like a record, and turning in circles. Each time he says "In other words," he makes the gesture.

In other words/ In other words/ In other words, *(etc.)*

Then wham! Another big FLASH stops the skipping and RICHIE gets to his feet, snapping on the fucker with the camera, still not being able to pinpoint exactly where it's coming from, but he makes for the audience to find him.

All right, that's it! I've fucking had it with you dude what is your fucking—

And he zaps into an electrified fence that separates him from the audience. Ow. The perimeter throbs with electricity.

A terrible silence. What?

He is unsure. So he carefully takes a finger and confirms that what he just hit was—

Zap!

No.

What is this place?

He looks around. He is trapped in a cell. He summons his courage and this time, with some might behind it, thrusts an arm at the "wall." A huge zap sends him pained to the floor.

He hears something. Coming from beyond his cell. He approaches a wall to listen. Very faintly we hear some lines from the opening jungle speech. He searches for where this is coming from. He goes to another wall and listens. Where we hear lines from later in the play.

On screen we see the "And they told two friends… and so on… and so on" thing from the montage; the effect being that there are countless cells with countless RICHIE EXCELLENTs *on every side of him, repeating this show over and over and over again.*

He panics. He tries to process. He breaks down. His mind is blowing.

My name's Richie Excellent cuz I have a good time. My name's Richie Excellent… cuz… I have a good time…

He ain't no Jedi; just a copy of some bullshit kid. Tears. Gagging tears.

I. am… the most major historical figure of the new millenium.

Finally, he looks at us, full of rage.

You. just. watched! What is this, *the zoo*?! Is that what this is? *Entertainment*? *(looking around, trying to locate himself)* Have I been here *forever*?

He tries to get it together.

It all happened to *him*. To the first… unless I am… I may never know… if I am him… or not. If I am the first, or second. This is REALLY FUCKING EMBARASSING, this is awful.

He forces a metaphysical exit:

There must have been a time *before* all this.

On screen, GENE, in bed, as at the beginning of the show:

GENE We move forward, that's what we do.

And screen out.

RICHIE talks himself through it.

RICHIE Before pen pals were extinct. Before trivia was conversational. And conversation was trivial. *(and lighting upon a certitude)* For I… recall… snowflakes… falling on my face after sticking the carrot in a snowman's head… all excited cuz tonight's the *Charlie Brown Christmas* special and Linus is once again gonna say some wicked stuff, and this hand-me-down snowsuit makes me sweat while I make an angel on the lawn… in the snow that was home… and always the feeling is of a terrible slowness overtaking haste.

He turns to us, defeated:

When you leave… which you will… do something for me. In winter's tedious nights, sit by the fire with good old folks, and let them tell thee tales of woeful ages long ago betid, and ere thou bid good night, to quite their griefs, tell thou the lamentable tale of me, and send the hearers weeping to their beds.

The mirror ball descends to him, ironic perfection, and he examines himself in it.

For there it is, cracked in a hundred shivers: one spirit spliced in a hundred and cast about the world. Is this the face of man? Or man unseated, given o'er the reins to's copy? At last outfaced by himself? Oh learn, good soul, to think our former state a happy dream, from which awaked, the truth of what we are shows us but this: I am *shared*. I am nothing. And having nothing, I am as ever before: insignificant, nameless, forgotten. *What do I do*?!

Why am I talking to you?! Put here with *toys*. Well take it! Take it all away!

The mirror ball flies away, he chucks away his lightsabre and knocks over his throne.

All in a flick of the metaphysical wand, all becomes nil and never was. What more remains?

Music. RICHIE gets to his feet.

Music do I hear!
Ha-ha! Keep time! How sour sweet music is
When time is broke, and no proportion kept;
So is it in the music of men's lives:
I wasted time, and now doth Time waste me.
This music mads me; let it sound no more!

The music does not stop but instead grows more disordered, more cacophonous. And will continue to grow this way to the end of the show.

Yet blessing on his heart that gives it me,
For 'tis a sign of love; and love to Richie
Is a strange brooch in this all-hating world.

FLASH! RICHIE is a dual personality.

That was so pretentious, man, can't believe you just spoke Shakespeare, ruined the whole suspension of disbelief thing / Forget that crap it died with digital / But there's an audience right there that paid good money to / They're not real / Sure they're real, say hello to the nice people, Richie / Hello, nice people!

FLASH! And RICHIE becomes a television announcer, America's Funniest Home Video*-style, and suffering intense pain, like his head is going to explode:*

All right then audience, let's check out those finalists! Will it be "Deathbed Doctor…"

On screen: GENE in bed.

GENE That humanity was wont to conquer this little world,
Hath made a shameful conquest of itself.

RICHIE Or will it be—

On screen we see RICHIE as the host of some cooking show. And simultaneously on stage and screen:

SCREEN AND STAGE RICHIE
We actually had time before the show to put together a complete thought, which should be simmering away in it's own juices just about ready to come out of the oven.

The screen goes out. RICHIE stumbles:

RICHIE We now return you to your regularly scheduled—

On screen: GENE in bed.

GENE Ah, would the scandal vanish with my life.
How happy then were my ensuing death.

RICHIE *(exactly as the opening line, but standing now)* Thanks for making the long drive out I know there were other parties n shit you will be remembered. Welcome.

FLASH! RICHIE is tossed onto the revolve. Shivering, bitterly cold, RICHIE offers a pathetic Teletubbies *farewell:*

Bye bye, Lala. Bye bye, Dipsy. I am the weakest link: goodbye.

On screen we see RICHIE walking down the hallway of a courthouse-looking building towards the front door. In this daydream he has decided NOT to go through with the procedure. We hear *CANDI Phurburger. This is the same scene we had earlier with CANDI, but from the POV of watching Richie.*

CANDI *(voice-over)* Mr. Excellent? Mr. Excellent?

We switch to RICHIE's POV… as we look out onto thousands of CANDI Phurburgers, countless clones, as far as the eye can see: Phurburger. Her voice is multiplied, echoey:

How do you feel, Mr. Excellent?

Horrified but keeping it all in, he ventures:

SCREEN RICHIE
Long live the king.

FLASH! The mother of all flashes. Everything gets amped up: music volume way up, RICHIE is freaking on stage, and on screen is a rapid firing off of images: symbols, slogans, inventions, technologies, ending with a shot of Darth Vader with his mask taken off, moments from death. Music out. We cut one last time to GENE, in bed, expiring, himself on his dying breath:

On stage, RICHIE resembles a newborn calf, trying to find his feet.

GENE We find out too late, as we always do, that all we looked for... was love.

Music back in, reaching a climax...

On screen we cut to the glowstick falling out of the girl's hand who got kicked out of Electric Circus. *We see her Starbucks coffee falling out of her other hand. She dropped it in order to take RICHIE's hand, who steps into frame. But—*

Wham! Back to the flashes of images on screen: noise, chaos, getting worse... now the images are of terrible tools, mass graves, war, sex, seals being clubbed, clear-cutting. Getting harsher and louder. Flashes. There is really way too much going on and this should be unbearably bright and loud. The audience is really uncomfortable.

RICHIE is now standing but in complete and utter agony, convulsing, hands pulling hair in some Blakean pose.

The screen image cuts to a blurry image of two little kids playing with toy lightsabres somewhere in the streets of suburbia. For this oh-so-brief bit, we hear a snippit of Joe Cocker's "A Little Help From My Friends," a Wonder

Years *moment: and then out as the film runs off the spool like a home movie.*

Silence. No screens. No music. Just RICHIE in a silent scream.

And then, released, calm, but throat fulla tears and shaky, RICHIE looks out at the audience.

RICHIE In other words… *(an arm outstretched)* Stop.

We hear the arctic wind sweep in as lights fade to black.

On screen: "LET'S BE CAREFUL OUT THERE."

And then it all fades away, perhaps to "snow," because the signal… is gone.

David Bowie's "The Man Who Sold the World" as the audience exits.

LITTLE DRAGON

BY KEIRA LOUGHRAN

KEIRA LOUGHRAN

Keira is a director, writer, actor, and theatre artist. She is the founding artistic director of K'Now Theatre, is Associate Director of Dramaturgy and New Plays at the Stratford Shakespeare Festival, and was Artistic Producer of the SummerWorks Theatre Festival from 2005 to 2007. She has worked for companies across the country, including Theatre Passe Muraille, Factory Theatre, Nightwood Theatre, fu-GEN Asian-Canadian Theatre Company, the Canadian Stage Company, Alberta Theatre Projects, Persephone Theatre, Roseneath Theatre, and Young Peoples' Theatre. *Little Dragon* is her first play, which she wrote, co-directed, starred in, and finally co-produced with Theatre Passe Muraille. That production received three Dora Mavor Moore Award nominations, including Outstanding New Play. Keira is a graduate of the University of Alberta's BFA Acting program. She has her black belt in aikido and currently lives in Stratford with her partner and new baby.

Little Dragon is my love child from China. For two months in 2001, I backpacked through the temples and fields of my ancestors and found that—unlike most Western travellers I encountered—this "backwards" country made complete sense to me; I felt surprisingly at home. For the first time, I relished the anonymity of disappearing in a crowd, I felt empowered belonging to such an unstoppable horde, and I experienced a pride of history and place that I had never found in Canada. It was an experience I hadn't planned for—I'd merely wanted to see a communist country in action. It ended up being a much-needed catalyst to that quintessential experience of coming-of-age. By finding pride and identity in my roots, I was finally able to question the world I had grown up in, and I discovered a story in that exploration.

At the same time, I was training intensely for my first *kyu* in aikido—one level short of my black belt. The lessons I was learning through this practice found their way into the script and inspired the physical world I wanted it to inhabit. Perhaps it was understandable; looking back on my childhood, many of the early shows I was taken to included feats of physical prowess—Chinese acrobats, ballets, figure skating, etc. These dynamic performances compelled me to experiment with an equally engaging physical and visual narrative that was woven into the story and told through tableaux, contact improvisation, and martial arts.

While *Little Dragon* is based on aspects of my life—I did grow up in North York in the eighties; I did go to a university that had little cultural diversity, making me more aware of my ethnicity; and I did once mistake a photo of Bruce Lee for my birth father, who died when I was very young—I hope I have found larger truths in the play that are couched in the details of Jen's story. In this country of immigrants, even those many generations back, the feeling of being an outsider is close to many of us. While sometimes painful, our work as artists is often made more vital by such an experience.

Bruce Lee is one such artist, becoming an iconic hero for Asian immigrants in North America. In writing *Little Dragon*, I was delighted to find so many connections between my experiences and those I found in his writings, most prominently in the book *Bruce Lee: Artist of Life*, compiled and edited by John Little and published by Tuttle Publishing. What began as an entertaining idea—being the long-lost daughter of the martial-arts superstar—took on greater resonance as I learned more about the man and discovered how much his musings and philosophies fit with my own and opened my mind further.

SummerWorks was the perfect birthing ground for my baby. Though I had not previously participated in the festival, I had been an avid audience member for years and thought it the best fit for the production I envisioned. I am indebted to then-artistic producer Franco Boni for his enthusiasm and support of the project right from the start. I met some of my closest friends and colleagues that summer and found my place in a real community. When I succeeded Franco as artistic producer of the festival in 2005, I felt once again at home. During my tenure, it remained my favorite part of the job—giving an artist I didn't really know the opportunity to do their first show and see it through to success. Creating a home for independent theatre artists where they could pursue their dreams on their own terms was my highest priority, as that was the greatest gift the festival afforded me.

The success of *Little Dragon* at SummerWorks was overwhelming. I was blessed with a brilliantly talented and dedicated cast and creative team, who threw themselves into the project and extracurricular aikido classes with heart and soul. I was also humbled by the innovation and vitality of the other shows in the festival—the range of vision and diversity of artists involved.

The subsequent development and two-act production of the piece remains a cornerstone in my development as an artist.

None of it would have been possible without the initial production at SummerWorks. This script is, appropriately, the one-act SummerWorks version, with only a few edits included from the two-act draft. I believe it best encapsulates the original line of questioning I set out to explore, and has a "simplicity of expression" which I think Bruce would appreciate. Enjoy!

—Keira Loughran

Little Dragon was first produced by K'Now Theatre as part of the 2002 SummerWorks Theatre Festival at Theatre Passe Muraille with the following company:

JEN	Keira Loughran
EUGE	Michelle Polak
COREY	Angela Besharah
GERALDINE	Jean Yoon
BRUCE/SENSEI	Richard Lee
Voice of MOM	Jane Luk

Directed by Keira Loughran & Marion de Vries
Stage managed by Chris Dupuis
Sound design by Lyon Smith
Lighting design by Trevor Schwellnus
Fight direction by Richard Lee
Produced by Derrick Chua

CHARACTERS

JEN	A third-generation Chinese-Canadian, first-year university student.
EUGE	Jen's friend. A funky Jewish girl also in first-year university.
COREY	Jen's roommate. A bright, perky girl from Truro, Nova Scotia.
GERALDINE	Jen's maternal grandmother. A second-generation Chinese-Canadian woman who aspired to WASPy upper-class acceptance.
SENSEI	Jen's aikido instructor.
BRUCE	Bruce Lee.

The actor who plays Bruce also plays Sensei. Other roles are secondary and are played by the core group of actors.

THE SETTING

The play takes place in Kingston, Ontario, in 1992–93. Locations rapidly shift between Jen and Corey's dorm room, Geraldine's house, the aikido dojo, Alfie's pub, and other campus locations. The staging of the play should be highly physical, reflecting both the martial art that Jen is studying and the shifting relationship dynamics that she is experiencing throughout her journey. A bare, matted stage accomplishes this most easily, also allowing the space to reflect Jen's psychological reality more than the physical reality.

Bruce's lines were inspired by the writings of Bruce Lee—particularly from his book *Bruce Lee: Artist of Life*, compiled and edited by John Little and published by Tuttle Publishing.

Michelle Polak, Richard Lee, and Keira Loughran; photo by Catherine Farquharson.

PROLOGUE

Spotlight comes up on JEN, centre stage, doing tai chi…

JEN I didn't realize I was Chinese until I went to university. I mean, I guess I had an inkling growing up, but it didn't mean anything; my friends ate with chopsticks as I well as I did, and we all had peanut butter and jam sandwiches for lunch. It was North York in the eighties. My classroom was a regular United Nations, all dutifully speaking Canada's two official languages.

I went to university in Kingston, Ontario. Queen's University, class of '96. Student number 1964321. An unknowing inmate of Kingston's sixth, but largely unrecognized, prison.

It was a year of trepidation. A year of exploration. A year of transformation. It was the year I discovered… *gung fu*!

A Chinese gong sounds.

JEN DISCOVERS AIKIDO

As JEN stands centre stage, EUGE rolls into her, having been thrown from off stage.

JEN Oh, I'm sorry!

EUGE bows to her, runs off stage, only to be thrown back on by her offstage partner. This happens a few times.

Um… excuse me…

EUGE Yeah?

JEN Um… I'm looking for a yoga class…? Do you know where…?

EUGE Yoga? Yeah, I think they're down the hall. 'Scuse me.

She runs off again and continues practising. JEN starts to leave but hesitates, drawn into the rhythm of the practise and the grace of the movement. When EUGE gets thrown at her again, she interrupts one more time…

JEN Um… I'm sorry.… What class is this?

EUGE It's a club—the Aikido Club…

SENSEI *(offstage)* Hei!

EUGE glances back to her partner, smiles apologetically to JEN, and returns to her partner. SENSEI enters.

Can I help you?

JEN *(awed)* Uh… um… no… that's okay. Thanks.

SENSEI returns to class. JEN watches him go.

JEN AND COREY

COREY enters. The girls are in their dorm.

COREY Jen! Jen, guess what?!

JEN What?

COREY Oh my God! I'm so excited!!!

JEN What is it?

COREY They just made me head of the Highland dance team!!!!

JEN Wow! That's great, Corey, congratulations.

COREY Can you believe it?! I can't believe it!! They said they don't usually give the position to a frosh, but because I have experience and the right kind of energy…

JEN That's totally great.

COREY Thanks!! Hey! How was yoga?

JEN Oh, I don't know—

COREY I had a boyfriend who was totally into yoga. He was a triathlete, and he said it helped him ground himself or something. Oh my God, I still can't believe it!!!

JEN Congratulations, Corey, that's really great.

COREY Hey, a bunch of us are going to Alfie's tonight to celebrate. You should totally come.

JEN Sure, sounds good.

COREY Oh my God, I have to tell Christy…

She runs out of the room.

(off) Christy? Christy! Guess what?! *(offstage whisper)*

GIRLS *(off)* OMIGOD!!!! / AHHHHHH!!!!!

JEN moves over to the answering machine. It's beeping. She picks up the message.

MOM *(voice-over)* Hi honey, it's Mom. Are you there? Oh, well I guess I missed you again; I just never know when to call.… Dave and I are having a wonderful time. There are so many birds here! Yesterday morning we went out on the balcony and there was this huge toucan sitting on the railing! It scared your father half to death! Well, anyway—

JEN fast-forwards through the message.

…and it was just cawing and cawing—caw, caw—it was just terr—

JEN fast-forwards through the message.

...so I asked what their neighbour's name was, and it turns out to be the same breeder we got the dogs from! Now isn't that a small world? Well, anyway—

JEN fast-forwards again.

...Okay, well, I guess I'll try you again later.... Are you there...? No, no, okay, never mind. I hope you're having fun and taking care of yourself. Okay, love you!

JEN erases the message.

JEN AND GRAM

GERALDINE *(off)* Jen? Is that you? Jen?

JEN Yeah, Gram, it's me. I'm a bit early—

GERALDINE *(entering)* You're early. Why are you so early? You're not supposed to be here for another twenty minutes.

JEN Sorry.

JEN kisses her gram, which GERALDINE receives grudgingly.

At least I'm not late this time...

GERALDINE Well... pfff... late is better than early... the tea isn't even ready yet. Let me just... you sit. I'll be back in a minute.

GERALDINE exits to the kitchen. JEN sits. She gets up and starts towards the kitchen.

JEN Can I help you with anything in there?

GERALDINE *(off)* No no! You just... sit. You're my guest.

JEN I'm your granddaughter.

GERALDINE You're my guest. Do you take milk or sugar?

JEN No, black is fine, thanks.

GERALDINE enters with tea and biscuits.

GERALDINE It's lovely to see you, sweetie, how's school going?

JEN I don't know. It's kind of overwhelming. I'm not really used to being on my own.

GERALDINE You sure you don't want milk at least?

JEN Um.... Sure. Thanks.

GERALDINE So, you were saying?

JEN Oh... um... nothing. My roommate was just named head of the Highland dance team.

GERALDINE Oh, I love those girls in their little kilts—is that the Blake girl?

JEN Yes, Corey.

GERALDINE Did you ask her if she's related to Arthur Blake? Arthur Blake used to own that big drugstore chain… what was it called…? Anyway, his father was a friend of your grandfather's from Vancouver.

JEN I doubt it then, Corey's from Truro, Nova Scotia.

GERALDINE Well, you never know. You'd meet lots of good people on the Highland dance team, Jen, they're at all the football games… unless you already have a special friend?

JEN Do you mean have I met a nice Chinese boy?

GERALDINE No! Chinese boys are no good. They're lazy and unreliable. Even your grandfather, God bless his soul. No, you need to find a nice Canadian boy who works hard and comes from a good family. Like your father—how is he doing?

JEN Dave? Fine, I guess. Mom and him are in Hawaii for a few months, didn't she tell you?

GERALDINE David is such a good man. A lot of men would have run far away from a single woman with a child—your mother is a lucky woman.

JEN Yeah, Dave's great.

GERALDINE I'm so glad you came to school here, Jen. Now I get to see you more—I'm not getting any younger, you know.

JEN Well, you don't look a day over forty.

GERALDINE Thank you, sweetie, I guess being Chinese is good in that respect. We do age well. Anyway, I've been doing some more clearing out and I found a few things that I thought you could use. *(She takes out a plastic bag full of junk.)* These are some magazines I thought you'd like. There's articles on Princess Diana and a clothing auction she did for charity. She is such a classy woman.

JEN *(unenthusiastically)* Yeah…

GERALDINE *(She pulls small sample-size shampoo bottles out of the bag.)* And here's some shampoo… from Italy. I took them from all the hotels your grandfather and I stayed in when we visited…

JEN It's okay, Gram, you don't need to—

GERALDINE Nonsense, they might as well get used by someone. I had some old tea towels too; now where did I put them…?

AT ALFIE'S

The gang enters, drunk and boisterous, while "Home for a Rest" plays in the background.

CHRIS Jennifer Macdonald?! Now how did a girl like you get a name like that?

STEVE Yeah Jen, where are you from, anyways?

JEN Me? Oh… ah… Toronto.

CHRIS No, but like, before that…

JEN I was born in Toronto…

STEVE No, but, where's your family from?

JEN They're from Toronto too—my mom grew up in Lawrence Park, and my dad—well, my second dad—grew up in Leaside.

COREY Your second dad?

JEN Yeah…

COREY What happened to your first dad?

JEN He, uh, he died before I was born…

COREY Oh my God! That's so sad.

JEN No, but it's okay, because my mom met Dave, and he's really great.

COREY Oh! That's how you got your name, I couldn't figure it out…

JEN Yeah…

CHRIS So what about your real dad, Jen? Where was he from?

JEN I don't know.

STEVE You don't know?

JEN No, I mean, I know he was Chinese, but—

STEVE Oh! So you're Chinese— *Ni hao.*

JEN Sorry?

STEVE *Ni hao.*

JEN I… I don't speak.

COREY You never learned?

JEN Um… no.

COREY Why not?

JEN I just… um… it's not a big deal.

STEVE I can say hello in six different languages: *Ni hao, Konicheewa, Anyong-ha say-yo—*

CHRIS Hey Jen, I heard if you say "I bought a horse" in Chinese in the wrong accent, it means "I fucked your mother"…

STEVE It's not the wrong accent, it's the wrong tone. Chinese is a tonal language, right Jen?

JEN I… wouldn't know.

CHRIS Jen, relax! You need to get drunk! Shouldn't be too hard. All the Orientals I know turn beet red after, like, one beer…

The song "I'm Gonna Be (500 Miles)" comes on.

COREY Omigod! I love this song!! Come on, guys, let's dance!!!

Everyone gets up and starts to jump up and down and sing along.

THE MORNING AFTER

JEN and COREY's dorm. COREY is collapsed on the floor.

JEN Corey... Corey... have you seen my keys?

COREY Hmmm? Oh, shit. What time is it?

JEN It's like, twelve thirty, I have to go to the library, and I can't find my keys.

COREY Morning checklist, let's see. *(She sits up and lies back down again.)* Oh shit. Check over there— *(She rolls over to reveal the keys underneath her.)*

JEN Got 'em.

COREY That was so much fun last night! Didn't you have a good time?

JEN *(beat)* Yeah, it was great.

COREY I think Steve thinks you're cute.

JEN Which one's Steve?

COREY Steve, you know Steve.... He's like this tall, curly brown hair? Great ass.

JEN Sorry, Corey, I'm discovering I've got this problem with white guys—they all look the same.

COREY You know... Steve...

JEN You're still drunk—go back to sleep...

COREY I wish I was still drunk, my head is killing me.

JEN MEETS EUGE

The library. JEN is trying to study. Sounds of klezmer-hip-hop music comes from the headphones of the girl beside her—Eugenia. JEN is at first slightly annoyed, but gets more intrigued by the funky-looking Jewish girl and the unique sounds coming through the headset.

JEN What are you listening to?

EUGE Oh! Sorry, am I disturbing you? *(She goes to turn it down.)*

JEN No! It sounds cool. I've just never heard it before.

EUGE It's klezmer hip hop.

JEN Klezmer?

EUGE Old Jewish gypsy music. My zaida used to listen to this shit all the time, but now it's been mixed with all these hip hop and industrial sounds. Wanna listen?

She offers up the headphones, which JEN puts on and listens to.

JEN I like it. It's a nice break from the usual stuff floating around here.

EUGE Yeah, if I hear "500 Miles" one more time, I'm going to tear open an artery.

JEN I know what you mean! I'm Jen.

EUGE Eugenia. My friends call me Euge.

JEN I've seen you before, are you in residence?

EUGE Yeah, Jean Royce. You?

JEN Ban Righ.

EUGE Ugh.

JEN Yeah, it's pretty gross. The food is shit, there's not even the idea of privacy…

EUGE That's why I chose Jean Royce: single rooms, kitchen facilities…

JEN West campus, though. It's pretty far out there.

EUGE Not far enough for me. Maybe if you head east on the highway another couple of hours…

JEN Montreal?

EUGE Yeeaahh… I love that city. I should have gone to McGill.

JEN Why didn't you?

EUGE These guys offered me more money. What can I say, I'm a whore.

JEN At least you have an excuse. I actually thought this place would be fun!

EUGE Well, it can be. If you go for homogenous mob

mentality partying, or if you're in a position to buy the whole "the world is ours and always will be" crap that's fostered here.

JEN So where do I know you from?

EUGE Didn't you come by my aikido club one day? A while ago?

JEN Nooo... yes. Yes I did. I was looking for yoga. That's right.

EUGE Did you find it?

JEN Yeah, but it didn't do it for me. The stuff you were doing looked pretty cool. What's it called again?

EUGE Aikido. It's a non-competitive, Japanese martial art. You should come check it out if you're interested. Learn to kick some ass...

JEN Didn't you just say it was non-competitive?

EUGE Yeah, but you still get to throw guys around, learn how to punch...

JEN Throw guys around? I hope you're speaking metaphorically...

EUGE Nope.

JEN Maybe I'll see you there.

JEN'S FIRST AIKIDO CLASS

SENSEI Punch.

JEN tries to punch. SENSEI untucks her thumb from her fist.

JEN Sorry.

SENSEI Don't apologize. Just watch and copy. Aikido is movement.

JEN Right, sorry—I mean… *(She cringes.)* sorry…

She punches again, weakly. SENSEI pats his centre. JEN aims for his belly, SENSEI moves off-line, JEN nearly falls over.

SENSEI Stay grounded when you attack, otherwise it's too easy to throw you.

JEN punches him, SENSEI performs a technique, throws JEN.

JEN Wow! HA!!!

SENSEI looks sharply at her while EUGE puts a finger to her lips. Oops. They bow to each other. A series of rolls to signify the class.

EUGE You made it.

JEN Barely.

EUGE No, you did good.

JEN I didn't even know how to make a fist—it was totally humiliating. That's what I get for being a pacifist all my life.

EUGE What did you do?

JEN shows her the errant thumb tucked under her fist.

JEN I thought my thumb would be more protected if it was tucked in.

EUGE Yeah, better protect those opposable thumbs—they're all you got going for you!

She play punches JEN, who ducks out of the way.

Well, you got the first step—get out of the way. What about the second?

She grabs JEN's wrist and locks it in nikkyo.

JEN Okay! Okay! *(She taps out.)* Jeez, it's only my first class!

EUGE You've never taken martial arts before? You did really good...

JEN Must be in the genes. It's fun! I like all the throws...

EUGE Yeah, wait till you learn breakfalls...

JEN Have you done any other martial arts?

EUGE I did some Indonesian stick fighting when I was there.

JEN You lived in Indonesia?

EUGE Yeah, for six months with Canada World Youth.

JEN Cool.

EUGE Yeah, it was a trip. Eye-opening, you know? Have you travelled much?

JEN Not much, I've been to Disney World.

EUGE Ugh.

JEN Yeah, kinda. I don't know, it was fun at the time.

EUGE Fuckin' headquarters of the Aryan race. Have you seen *Aladdin*?

JEN Yeah!

EUGE Did you ever notice how Aladdin turned more white as the movie went on?

JEN Uh…

EUGE Fuckin' offensive!

JEN …Yeah!

EUGE It's nice to have another girl in the class. Hey, you doing anything now? You wanna go for a drink?

JEN Um… I'm supposed to— No! I'd love to.

JEN AND COREY

COREY — Jen, where were you? You missed the game!

JEN — I'm sorry, Corey, I met this girl at my class—

COREY — It was my first game as head of the team!

JEN — I know, I'm sorry. I'll come to the next one, I promise—

COREY — We're not playing another home game for like three weeks! I really could have used the support, you know!

JEN — I'm really sorry, Corey, I just—I lost track of time. Did you win?

COREY — No. The boys sucked. But we were totally amazing! The girls looked great!

JEN — Congratulations. I'm sorry I missed it.

COREY — That's okay. Oh, hey, your mom called—did you call her back last time?

JEN — Um… I don't know.

COREY — Your mom's so nice! She just wanted to let you know they got back safe from Hawaii—it sounds like they had a wonderful time. Get her to tell you about the monkeys! She'll be home all night, you should give her a call.

JEN — Sure, thanks Corey.

COREY — My parents never go anywhere. They don't trust big cities I think. Oh hey! I was right, Steve was asking about you today after the game. I told him you'd come to Alfie's tonight.

JEN — I don't know if I can, Corey, I'm meeting a friend.

COREY — Who? A boy?

JEN — No, just this girl Euge.

COREY — Well, bring her along!

JEN — I don't know. I'll see. She's helping me with a paper.

COREY — What's it for?

JEN — I have to come up with my personal thesis on the nature versus nurture argument.

COREY — Oh.

JEN — I mean, which do you think is more definitive in establishing your character: nature or nurture?

COREY — I don't know… nature?

JEN — It's not multiple choice, Corey—oh, don't worry about it.

COREY — Well, I don't know about nature/nurture or whatever, but I think that people are generally kind and will give back what you put out. Do unto others, you know?

JEN — Right.

COREY Aren't you going to call your mom?

JEN Later.

JEN AND GRAM

JEN and GERALDINE are having tea.

GERALDINE It's too bad you didn't come earlier. Doctor Phillips was here. He's an old friend of the family. He was your mother's GP when she was a girl.

JEN He lives in Kingston?

GERALDINE No, no, he was just passing through. He's going to visit his son Malcolm. You know, Malcolm was sweet on your mother for quite some time. She missed her chance on that one, all right.

JEN Gram!

GERALDINE It's true! Malcolm is one of the top architects in the country! More tea?

JEN I started taking aikido, Gram.

GERALDINE What's that?

JEN I started taking aikido. It's a Japanese martial art.

GERALDINE Pfff... Japanese... what do you need that for?

JEN It's really interesting, Gram. It means "The Way of Harmony," and the idea is that you blend with your opponent's energy and redirect his attack back onto him. Very Zen.

GRAM doesn't respond.

It's based in traditional forms like ju-jitsu and stuff. But it's cool because it's all about channelling the power of the universe, so it doesn't matter how big you are or if you're a man or a woman, anyone can practise and be just as good.

GRAM still doesn't respond.

So, I've been going like, three times a week. It's really good exercise, and my sensei is really impressed. He says if I keep up regularly, I can test for my fifth *kyu* before the end of the year.

GERALDINE Why don't you take one of those step classes? Florence's niece teaches them at the YMCA; they're very good to tone your tush!

JEN Yes, well, aikido's very good for your abs—

GERALDINE That Highland dancing would be good exercise too, you know…

JEN You know what, Gram? I have to get going. I'm meeting a friend.

GERALDINE Who?

JEN Just my friend Euge. Eugenia.

GERALDINE What kind of name is that?

JEN She's Jewish, Gram. I'll bring her over sometime.

GERALDINE Jewish, pfff. I still haven't met your other friend, the Blake girl. I still think she might be related to Arthur.

JEN Right.

GERALDINE Oh, and before you go, I have more things for you… here's some nylons… they've got some runs but they're still good as an extra layer…

JEN Sure…

GERALDINE And, oh! These are some articles I thought you might like to read. They're about your Uncle Sanford—you remember Uncle Sanford? He's head of one of those big software companies now!

JEN Yeah. Thanks Gram. I'll see you soon.

GERALDINE Bye, dear, see you next week.

AIKIDO

JEN and EUGE are practising shomenuchi. *SENSEI walks by. JEN does* shomen, *but she is too far away.*

SENSEI *(shakes his head)* You're too far away. Even if you try to hit, you'll miss your target.

He stands to be her partner and nods to practise. She strikes towards his head but is too far. SENSEI pulls her hand to where it should land. She nods and strikes again, closer this time, but stopping mid-air as he moves off-

line. She looks at him, puzzled. He pushes her arm down—follow through. Right. She strikes at him one more time, and this time hits him square on the head.

JEN Oh my god! I'm so sorry!

SENSEI It's your job to try to hit the target. It's my job to get out of the way. That was good. Continue.

EUGE and JEN continue to practise while SENSEI supervises. Others practise in the back.

You mustn't be afraid of your goal. Engage with your partner. If you do not connect with her, there is no practise, there is no Way. If you are thrown, get back up and engage again.

EUGE This is exhausting!

JEN Yeah, but isn't it great?

A series of rolls over obstacles and each other to signify class, with other cast members joining in as other students. At the end they all bow to each other and say thank you in Japanese.

BRETT *(as he bows to JEN)* You're really good. Have you been practising long?

JEN Oh, no, not really. You?

BRETT I've got my black belt in tae kwon do, but I just started aikido. I'm Brett.

JEN *(shakes his hand)* Jen.

BRETT Nice to meet you. Hey—what are you saying when you bow?

JEN Oh, just… "thank you for practising" in Japanese.

BRETT No, but, how do you say it?

JEN Um… well, I say "*arigato gozaimashita*"… but I'm not really sure I'm pronouncing it…

BRETT "*Arigato gozaimashita*"?

JEN Yeah, but you might want to check it with Sensei or someone who speaks Japanese.

BRETT "*Arigato gozaimashita*"… and what's the other one, that you say before you practise?

JEN Um… I say "*onigashimasu*," but again…

BRETT "*Onigashimasu*"…

EUGE It means, "Please practise with me."

BRETT *(looking at JEN)* "*Onigashimasu*," "*arigato gozaimashta*"—thanks. I'll see you next class.

He leaves.

EUGE Fucking Rice King.

JEN What?

EUGE Nothing.

JEN It's so weird, Euge. People are starting to look to me to help them with their technique and shit.

I've only been practising for a few months!

EUGE Yeah, well, you're Asian. You've got that credibility thing.

JEN What do you mean?

EUGE Look, Jen, you're Asian, you're a woman, you're in a martial-arts class, and you're tough. That's very sexy.

JEN But I'm so not! I'm totally normal! You make me sound exotic or something.

EUGE Yeah, that's why they get confused; you don't fit in their box. They think you should be one thing because of how you look, and when you prove to be something else it just shortwires their brains.

JEN It is kind of fun sometimes though. I mean, they really listen to me. I'm just quoting Sensei, but it really seems to help. Maybe it is stupid that I don't know anything about Asian culture. I should learn more about martial arts and stuff.

EUGE Fine, but don't do it for them, do it for yourself. Your problem, Jen, is that you're scared to be different. You have to realize that you are different, and quite frankly, your uniqueness is what makes you interesting.

JEN It's not that I don't want to be Chinese, I just don't know how to be Chinese. What am I supposed to do? Eat lots of rice? Drive badly?

EUGE Don't be stupid. It's just something you know. It's in your blood. Your family.

JEN	My family? *(beat)* So I can't just get, like, a yin-yang tattoo on my ass and call it a day?
EUGE	Do you have a Chinese name? You could do characters!
JEN	No, I hate it.
EUGE	What, your name? What is it?
JEN	It sounds stupid. I don't know, it means "Little Dragon." I guess it's 'cause I'm a Scorpio.
EUGE	How do say your name in Chinese?
JEN	No. Forget it. It's dumb.

JEN AND GRAM

JEN	Gram, how did our family get here?
GERALDINE	Oh Jen, our family has been here for generations.
JEN	But how did we get here in the first place, from China? Was it the railroad?
GERALDINE	No! We weren't coolies. Our family were wealthy merchants back in Canton. Now, I found my old crochet needles and thought I might teach you—
JEN	Did you ever send Mom to Chinese school?
GERALDINE	No. You start with a slip knot—
JEN	Why not?

GERALDINE It's really quite simple—

JEN Gram—why not?

GERALDINE Well, she never asked, and besides, she was learning English at school.

JEN Why didn't you speak it at home?

GERALDINE Why bother? She never would have used it. Chinese is a hard and useless language in Canada.

JEN Well, I think it's a shame. I don't know anything about where I come from.

GERALDINE Jennifer Macdonald, you are Canadian. You were born here, your mother was born here, I was born here.

JEN But what about China? If we don't continue our cultural heritage, who will?

GERALDINE Jen, I don't know any more about China or Chinese culture than I know about… about… Zimbabwe! Do you know how much China has changed since my mother left? Why hang on to a culture that no longer exists?

JEN I just think there's something there that I should know about. Everyone already expects me to.

GERALDINE Don't waste your time. The Chinese are a backwards race who have isolated themselves for so long that they can no longer catch up to the rest of the world. They want everything their way and have no respect or tolerance for differences. I don't want to talk about this anymore. More tea?

JEN *(beat)* Actually, I have to get going. I have class.

GERALDINE On a Sunday?

JEN Aikido class. My martial art.

Beat.

GERALDINE Well, if you have to go.... I found a box of your mother's old things in the closet.

JEN Gram, I...

GERALDINE I haven't looked through it. It's probably just old books or toys, but I thought you might give it to her when you go home.

JEN Gram, you keep giving me all this crap—

GERALDINE Jennifer!

JEN *(beat)* I'm sorry. I'm so sorry, Gram. I didn't mean to be rude. Of course I'll take mom's things. Thank you.

YIN YANG

Split scene: EUGE meets COREY / JEN looks in the Box.

EUGE Jen?

COREY Hi! Jen's not in right now.

EUGE Oh! Um. I was supposed to meet her here at two. I'll come back.

COREY That's okay, you can wait here, I'm sure she'll be back soon. I'm Corey.

EUGE Eugenia.

COREY Oh! You're Euge! It's nice to finally meet you!

EUGE Thanks.

Pause. JEN pulls out a black belt, a dragon knife…

COREY Well, here, make yourself comfortable. Do you want some tea or something?

EUGE That's okay. Thanks.

Uncomfortable pause. JEN pulls out a book by Bruce Lee.

JEN *Bruce Lee Papers…*

BRUCE enters upstage behind JEN.

EUGE Congratulations on the Highland dance team…

COREY Thanks! Do you go to a lot of games?

EUGE No.

JEN starts reading from the book.

JEN/BRUCE The Chinese concept of *yin yang* is integral to the artful practice of *gung fu*. Seemingly opposite and disjunctive, they are in fact defined by each other, through each other; existing only together as an indivisible whole.

EUGE — I think spectator sports are the lowest type of activity. They're manipulative, mind-numbing, pseudo-intelligent diversions that maintain the status quo by allowing organized catharsis. It's so Greco-Roman.

COREY — *(beat)* Yeah, I wasn't really into sports before this.... Well, I used to do like track and stuff, and my dad was really into football, so I guess I kinda fell into it. *(laughs nervously)*

EUGE — Well, if you're actually playing it's okay, it's just the whole oogi, oogi, oogi thing that I can't stand.

COREY — Right.

Uncomfortable pause. JEN leafs though the book and continues reading.

JEN/BRUCE — While the Western man thinks of two forces: yin *and* yang, the Chinese man knows it to be one principle; reflected in every aspect of the natural world—the changing of the seasons, the flowing of the tide. The *gung-fu* man who unites himself with this unstoppable truth is unstoppable himself...

EUGE — I could just wait in the common room—

COREY — No. It's no problem.

Standoff. JEN sits, something's pulling her brain, BRUCE hands her an old, worn photo of her father. She compares it to the photo on the back of Bruce Lee's book. She gasps—gong…

JEN Oh my God!

COREY So… Eugenia…. That's an interesting name, where does it come from?

EUGE My father's name is Eugene—my parents wanted a boy. Did that happen to you too?

COREY Nnoooo…

EUGE Where does Corey come from then?

COREY Um, I think it's Irish…

EUGE Oh! Do you speak Gaelic?

COREY umm… no… umm…

EUGE You know, I've always wanted to kiss the Blarney Stone. And you guys sure know how to drink!

COREY Uh…

JEN enters with the box. She is a bit out of sorts.

JEN Hi. Sorry I'm late, Euge. I… uh… I got stuck at my grandma's. You've met Corey.

EUGE/COREY Yeah.

JEN Okay, well, ready to go? *(EUGE nods, staring at COREY.)* Okay. *(to COREY)* See ya!

BIRTHRIGHT

EUGE and JEN outside, walking.

EUGE — So that's Corey.

JEN — Don't, Euge. She means well. She's just a bit...

EUGE — Dumb.

JEN — She's just a bit... out there.

EUGE — Jen, you and I are "out there." Doug Henning and the Natural Law Party are "out there." Corey and the Highland dance team and Queens University are definitely not considered "out there" by the majority of the population. I don't know why you waste your time with them.

JEN — It's not like they're bad people...

EUGE — You're too nice. People like that make me sick. They have it so easy and they take it completely for granted. They shit on people all the time without even realizing it, and if something doesn't fit into their narrow box of a world view, they dismiss it as unimportant and go on their merry way.

JEN — Come on, Euge, Corey's my roommate. I can't just ignore her.

EUGE — Why not? They ignore me!

JEN — Look, people are people. Maybe they can't help the way they think any more than you can. And if our souls are all connected to a greater power—

EUGE I'm an existentialist. I don't buy that shit.

JEN What do you mean?

EUGE You said you're a Scorpio? You're supposed to have the power of Pluto at your disposal! It's your birthright!

JEN My birthright… hm…. Have you ever heard of Bruce Lee?

EUGE Duh, of course, he's only the greatest martial artist who ever lived. Why?

JEN I, uh… I just got a copy of one of his books. I don't know… it really speaks to me.

EUGE They're actually making a movie about his life, it's coming out soon. We should totally go see it!

JEN *(mocking her)* Totally!!! You sound like Corey…

EUGE Fuck off, it's supposed to be good.

JEN Fuck you, fine.

MEDITATING

JEN is trying to meditate. The voice of Bruce Lee is going through her brain. BRUCE works with nunchucks behind her.

BRUCE *(voice-over)* Chinese *gung fu* is more than a physical practice; it is a spiritual discipline to be mastered over a lifetime. It is learned through surrender rather than strength of will. Like a garden, one can only work to create the right space for it to blossom and grow...

In the hallway, boppy music starts blaring.

JEN Fuck!

She gets up and yells out the door.

Turn your fucking music down!

She sits back down in front of her candle and tries again.

BRUCE *(voice-over)* The philosophy of *gung fu* is the philosophy of Taoism, of Zen. Energy is not good or bad, it simply *is*, and all energy strives for balance. There is no attack to resist, there is no fight to win, there is only movement, and being in harmony with that movement.

The phone starts to ring. JEN tries to ignore it.

The practice of *gung fu* is a physical practice of nature's laws and principles; an investigation into the essence of nature itself.

The answering machine has come on.

MOM *(voice-over)* Hi honey, just seeing if you're in. I guess you're busy with classes...

JEN hesitates—should she talk to her mom? Abruptly, she disconnects the answering machine. Settles back down.

BRUCE *(voice-over)* Be like the nature of water; ever-flowing, ever-penetrating, translucent, and unbreakable.

COREY enters and turns on the light. Sees JEN and starts.

COREY Oh! My God, you scared me! What are you doing?

JEN I'm trying to meditate but there's so much going on that I can't think straight.

COREY Isn't meditation about clearing your mind and not thinking at all?

JEN *(beat)* …shut up.

COREY Look, sorry to interrupt, but I have to get ready for a date. Jeff's taking me to see *Jurassic Park*.

JEN Didn't you just see it with… what's his name?

COREY Cameron, yeah, but Jeff doesn't know that and it's a great date movie! Scary and exciting, you know.

JEN Right.

COREY Besides, it was either that or *Aladdin*, and I figure he'd prefer the former.

JEN Do you know that Aladdin keeps getting whiter as the movie goes on?

COREY Sorry?

JEN Nothing. Never mind.

AIKIDO

JEN and EUGE are practising. SENSEI watches.

SENSEI — Be at the centre of an infinite circle. Move. Don't think. Get beyond yourself.

SENSEI walks away.

JEN — I think I was meant to take aikido, Euge. It's a natural progression.

EUGE — From what?

JEN — Well, Bruce Lee said that *gung fu* was essentially the idea of being harmonious with the force of the opponent. And what can be more harmonious than an art that translates to "The Way of Harmony"?

EUGE — What about jeet kun do? Wasn't that Bruce Lee's ultimate martial art?

JEN — Yeah, but there are lots of similarities between aikido and jeet kun do.

EUGE — Like what? Bruce Lee was totally against rigid styles and classical forms, and aikido is totally about classical forms.

SENSEI — Shhht!

JEN — Aikido uses classical forms, but, like jeet kun do, the ultimate goal is formlessness. I'll bet Bruce just didn't know about aikido, it would have been really new still when he was alive.

EUGE Bruce Lee would have known about aikido, he was on the cover of *Black Belt* magazine practically every month.

JEN Well then I'm sure Bruce recognized that aikido is just another way to the same goal. Another finger pointing at the moon. Bruce said—

EUGE I love how you're on a first-name basis with him now—

JEN BRUCE SAID—that *gung fu* was at the centre of all martial arts, so it would include Japanese martial arts as well.

EUGE I dare you to tell that to Sensei...

JEN Seriously, Euge, I think Bruce would like aikido as a practice. I think he would approve of my taking it.

EUGE Which is important because...?

JEN I mean, aikido is a form of *gung fu*, and jeet kun do is primarily a philosophical approach to *gung fu*, so I can practise aikido as a style with a jeet kun do approach to try to reach the moon.

She applies a technique abruptly in her enthusiasm.

EUGE Ow!

JEN Sorry.

EUGE I think you're mixing your metaphors.

SENSEI claps his hands to end practise.

Hey, we still on tonight for *Dragon*?

JEN You bet!

DRAGON: THE BRUCE LEE MOVIE

BRUCE leaps across the stage à la Dragon *poster image. JEN and EUGE come out of the movie theatre.*

EUGE What an excellent movie!

JEN What?!

EUGE I mean, I knew he was this awesome fighter, but I didn't realize how much adversity he had to overcome in his lifetime.

JEN But it wasn't accurate! I mean, Bruce was never paralyzed, just bedridden for a few months. And all that crap about being chased by his father's old demons? Come on…

EUGE I thought it was cool. That racist shit really gets me though. That scene when he doesn't get served at the restaurant because he's Chinese? I would have decked the guy.

JEN But Bruce would have contained himself. The *gung fu* man never asserts himself against his opponent.

EUGE What about his wife? She was so strong! I mean, he may have been the fighter, but it was totally obvious she was the real strength in the family.

JEN Come on, Euge. That whole love story was just Hollywood glamour. Bruce Lee didn't need anybody! The movie made him seem almost pathetic at times. They just didn't trust that they could sell a movie with a true Chinese hero—they needed the white girl to legitimize it or make it accessible. I mean, that's such bullshit!

EUGE I don't think they did that; remember all that stuff where he talked about being like nature and shit. That's totally Asian. And when he put the mirrors by the windows to scare the demons away…

JEN Yeah great, all the Chinese superstitious crap! You should really read his books, Euge. I mean, the stuff he talks about makes so much sense to me!

EUGE Ancient Chinese secrets?

JEN Fuck off! He's revolutionary, Euge. Like in an if-everyone-could-understand-what-he-was-saying-we'd-have-world-peace kind of way. It's just tragic that his death came right before he hit superstardom in North America.

EUGE *(joking)* I guess the world just wasn't ready for him.

JEN *(seriously)* I guess not. Still, maybe it's not too late…

JEN AND COREY

BRUCE enters—he is like JEN's guardian angel. Or at least her imaginary friend.

COREY You wanna go to AJ's tonight? It's Mark's birthday.

JEN Isn't it your birthday, like, tomorrow?

COREY Yeah, but we're going out for that on Friday. You have to come then.

JEN Okay, but I can't come tonight, I'm going to aikido.

COREY Oh my God! They opened an Ikea in Kingston?

JEN AikiDO. My martial-arts class?

COREY Oh, right. I always think you're saying Ikea. So, how's it going?

JEN It's amazing. You know, it feels so natural. Like it's in my blood.

COREY I had a boyfriend who was really into martial arts. He studied for like ten years or something.

JEN Was he Chinese?

COREY No. But he was totally into Chinese stuff. He always made me watch reruns of *Kung Fu*. We loved David Carradine.

JEN David Carradine's not Chinese. He's not even Asian.

COREY Oh. Well, he might as well be.

JEN You know, he stole that role from Bruce Lee.

COREY Really?

JEN Yeah. The studio was worried Bruce Lee looked too Chinese.

COREY Maybe David Carradine was just better.

JEN Have you ever seen Bruce Lee?

COREY I don't know. I mean, I've heard of him. He was in *The Green Hornet*, right?

JEN Yeah, he was Kato.

COREY Oh. I thought Kato was a horse.

JEN No. Kato was Bruce Lee.

COREY Yeah, well, I didn't really watch that show. But David Carradine—

JEN Fuck! Corey?!!

COREY What?

JEN Did you not hear anything I said? I mean… Jesus! You don't get it! Do you ever consider the racial implications of what you're saying?

COREY I'm sorry, I didn't mean—

JEN I know, you didn't mean anything, you never mean anything, but you know what? It does mean something, or at least it should. Oh, I'm sorry, is this confusing to you?

Beat.

COREY Fuck you!

Gong—they fight. COREY Highland-flings her way, dodging and deflecting JEN's attacks with surprising ease. JEN doesn't fare so well…

JEN Excuse me?

COREY I have gone out of my way to be good to you! I introduce you to all my friends and invite you in on all the stuff we do—

JEN Oh—thank you!

COREY No—now you're insulting me by suggesting what, exactly?

JEN Forget it. It's not worth it.

COREY No—I want to know. You think I'm stupid? You think I'm racist?

JEN Sometimes, yeah! *(Beat. COREY stops.)* I'm sorry, Corey, but there are a lot of things that you have never experienced, and probably never will, which make you… unaware and… insensitive to certain realities. I don't think it's your fault exactly, but I do think it's a fact.

COREY You know, Jen, I like you. We all do. And maybe I don't get it right all the time, but at least I try.

JEN Why? So you can brag about your one Chinese friend and feel better about yourself?

COREY See, that's the kind of stuff I'm talking about! You don't even try! If anyone is being racist, Jen, you are!

JEN Well, maybe it's about time. *(She pulls out the photo and studies it.)*

COREY Why do you think I came to this school, Jen? I know there's things I don't know about. I know there's more to learn. So I'm sorry I offended you, but you know, you don't have to be so rude. You can just tell me next time. *(Beat. JEN says nothing.)* Are we cool?

JEN *(not listening, still engaged with the photo)* ...Yeah...

COREY You're still coming to my birthday thing, right?

JEN ...What? Oh... sure.

COREY *(glances at the photo)* Who's that?

JEN Bru—my dad.

COREY Cu-ute!

AIKIDO

JEN is tossing EUGE around. She is getting stronger, more powerful, but she is not using EUGE's energy—she's asserting her own.

EUGE Hey tiger, what's with you today?

JEN I'm not a tiger, I'm a dragon. Little Dragon. Did you know that Bruce Lee's nickname was "Little Dragon" when he was a kid? Siu Loong…

EUGE Yeah well, Little Dragon, cool off a bit. I want to be able to practise tomorrow.

They continue to practise. SENSEI comes over and watches.

SENSEI You are not connecting with your partner. You practise alone.

JEN What do you mean?

SENSEI You think too much of yourself. Your technique has no flexibility.

He attacks JEN. She begins to perform the technique but SENSEI counterattacks and nearly elbows her in the head.

You see?

JEN offers her wrist. SENSEI takes it and again JEN starts the technique, more carefully this time. SENSEI resists and JEN can't move him.

Let go of your mind. Let go of your Self.

He guides her energy so the technique is effective.

Move. Be there, be not there.

JEN finishes the technique.

Surprise yourself. Blend. Harmony.

They bow to each other. EUGE and JEN continue to practise. He leaves. JEN goes back to her tough practise and throws EUGE hard.

JEN It works better the other way.

EUGE Uh—what happened to my turn?

JEN AND GRAM

JEN Gram, I never thanked you for that box of Mom's you gave me. All that Bruce Lee stuff? Why didn't you tell me Mom was into *gung fu*?

GERALDINE What are you talking about?

JEN It's okay, Gram—I know who he is. I've been reading his stuff and I've learned more from him than I've learned all year in school! It's something I've always known inside, I've just never had the words before. Thank you.

GERALDINE Oh, Jennifer, you still don't see?! All that kung-fu business is dangerous! Your mother, mooning after some boy, starts to take it, and at first it's all Tao this and Confucius that, and next thing I know she's lost all sense of herself! Idealistic fool! I told her! Chinese philosophy—pfff!

JEN Chinese philosophy is beautiful! The idea of belonging to something greater? Understanding the unity of all things; true and false, good and bad, right and wrong? Chinese culture is beautiful and you've rejected it at every turn. No wonder Mom left home; there was no room for her natural instincts. How can you turn your back on your own people?

GERALDINE Just because I don't talk like a fortune cookie I'm turning my back on my people?! And just who are my people, Jennifer Macdonald? The Chinese who hung on to their culture, who stayed thinking they were Chinese after they left China? They are the ones who are still selling bok choy in Chinatown and working for minimum wage. Those are not my people. The smart ones left China behind a long time ago and have worked to make room for themselves among their fellow Canadians in business and politics. Those are my people, Jennifer, and I have never turned my back on them. If you want to talk about turning your back, talk to your mother!

JEN What do you mean?

GERALDINE And if you want to talk about Chinese values, talk about family. Family duty and responsibility and respecting your elders!

JEN Gram—

GERALDINE I just wanted what was best for her; a good man, a good family, but she was determined to "follow her heart." And look where it got her. I tried to warn her but she wouldn't listen.

JEN Gram, calm down—

GERALDINE He broke her heart! She shows up on my doorstep with you in one arm and an empty purse in the other, and all she'll tell me is that she spent all her money on airfare back from Hong Kong.

JEN Hong Kong?

GERALDINE But do I ask questions? No, I don't turn my back on family.

JEN Oh my God.

JEN AND EUGE

JEN swoons. BRUCE picks her up and carries her into the next scene.

EUGE Hey Jen, where did you get this photo?

JEN It's my dad.

EUGE Jen, this is a picture of Bruce Lee.

JEN I know. He's my father.

EUGE What the hell are you talking about?!

JEN I know it sounds crazy, but listen, I found this photo when I was a kid, and I just knew it was my father. Then when I saw Bruce's photo on the back of his book, I figured it out!

EUGE Jen—

JEN No, listen. First, my Chinese name—Siu Loong?

Little Dragon? Second, my mom told me that my father died the year I was born—1973. The year Bruce Lee died? 1973.

EUGE You've got to be kidding—

JEN Also, my mom did her undergrad in Seattle, so she could've met Bruce there! And she was in Hong Kong when he died!

EUGE What about Linda Lee?

JEN Well, Bruce would have been a nobody when he met my mom, and she would have been forbidden to see him because Gram didn't want her to marry a Chinese guy. It totally makes sense!

EUGE So, what, you're the illegitimate daughter of Bruce Lee?

JEN *(beat)* Well, more like a love child, I think. Look, I know he was married and everyone always talks about how happy they were and all, but it doesn't add up. I mean, I've read all the stuff she wrote about him and, not to be mean, but she sounds pretty dumb.

EUGE Jen!

JEN No, I mean, I can understand why he married her in the first place; she was the perfect trophy bride for a young, ambitious Bruce: white, adoring, docile… the all-American girl.

EUGE But…?

JEN But as time went on, it wasn't enough. He needed a real partner. A Chinese woman who understood him, who was as strong as he was, and could match his fire.

EUGE Your mother.

JEN Just think, Euge: I am the only true Chinese descendant of Bruce Lee. He needs me. I'm the only one who can carry on his legacy.

EUGE Yeah, I think Shannon and Brandon might have something to say about that.

JEN CALLS MOM

JEN goes to the phone and calls her mom.

MOM *(voice-over)* Hi, hi! We're not home right now, please leave a message!

JEN Hi Mom. It's me. I'm just calling because… well… I mean, Gram gave me a box of your stuff. Your Bruce Lee stuff? And I… um… well, I figured… uh… I mean, I have this photo from… I just…. Mom, is Bruce Lee my…? *(She stops as she sees BRUCE. She recovers.)* I mean, is Bru—? *(The sight of him stops her again.)* …Just, call me.

She hangs up and looks at BRUCE.

I just know it's true. I know it in my blood, the very essence of my being. It just makes sense. It makes everything right. And just you wait, when people find out, they're gonna go nuts. They're gonna feel so bad about how they treated you that they're gonna love me. And I will teach them the Way; the Chinese way. I'll point my finger to the moon and when they look up at me, I'll say, "Please don't take my finger to be the moon or fix your eyes on my finger, for you will miss all the heavenly glory." And everyone will see. And understand. And feel blessed that they have this second chance. I will fulfill your legacy.

AT ALFIE'S

CHRIS I mean, it's so stupid! They already speak English…

JEN What's going on?

COREY Chris has to take Japanese next year as part of his business degree.

JEN So what's the big deal?

CHRIS Besides the fact that I suck at languages, it's the principle of the thing! Why should I be forced to learn a language I have no need for? I refuse to support a system that is trying to accommodate every Tom, Dick, and Tamaguchi!

JEN Excuse me?

CHRIS America leads the economic world. Everyone knows that and everyone deals with that by learning English. This fucking language class could sink my whole GPA! If we stand our ground, we keep our power. The Japs have already cornered the market on electronics and they're pushing for automotive control... somebody's got to stop them, let them know we're not going to start measuring the world's capital by the fucking Yen!

JEN Are you trying to be a bigot, Chris, or is it just natural?

COREY Jen—

JEN Japan has a beautiful culture and history that you could actually learn a hell of a lot from if you'd just open your eyes a bit.

CHRIS You've gotten feisty since you started your little kung-fu thing, eh Jen?

JEN Don't talk to me like that you sorry piece of shit. I could kick the crap out of you if I wanted to.

CHRIS Oooo, yeah, whip me good, baby...

COREY Chris—

CHRIS *(gives best Bruce Lee imitation kung fu ki-ai)* Hwahhh!

JEN punches CHRIS square in the face. Lights shift as the shocked crowd fades out and the shocked JEN takes focus.

NIGHTMARE SCENE

BRUCE Lee emerges from the shadows where CHRIS has just fallen. We hear cheesy Hong Kong action-movie music and are transported into a kung-fu movie.

BRUCE *(voice-over)* Siu Loong, you have insulted me, my family, and the spirit of Jeet Kun Do.

JEN Bruce?

BRUCE Only my friends may call me by my first name! You are no friend of mine!

JEN I'm your daughter…

BRUCE Look into your heart, Siu Loong…

JEN No! I just want to continue your work! You don't understand—I understand you. I know I do. Let me prove it to you.

BRUCE You want to prove it to me? Okay…. Hit me.

JEN What?

BRUCE Hit me.

They square off, JEN not sure if he's joking or not. She finally throws a punch. He stops her mid-attack with a kick that she narrowly avoids. Incensed, she pushes down his foot and punches again and again. He parries easily, grabs her hand, and throws her over his hip. She falls.

Come on, hit me again!

JEN Wait…! You hit me.

BRUCE sighs, readies himself, and punches JEN. She tries to perform a technique but he counterattacks and throws her down.

BRUCE Come on, Little Dragon, where's your fire now? Didn't realize you were stealing mine, did you?

JEN, angry, runs at BRUCE. She punches him: left, right, backfist. He parries all of them and starts to kick her butt.

It is not for you to continue my work; you must continue your own work! Self-knowledge is the basis of jeet kun do—Art is the expression of the Soul.

JEN But I'm trying—

BRUCE If you try, you have already failed. *(like Yoda)* Do or do not; there is no try.

JEN What—? Bruce…

He throws her down and continues to kick her butt.

BRUCE *(like an old Hong Kong movie)* You killed my master, now you must die!

JEN Huh?

BRUCE *(like Yul Brynner)* Head must not be higher than king's!

JEN But—

BRUCE *(like Darth Vader)* Jen… I am your father.

JEN Stop teasing me!

BRUCE *(in bad Chinese accent)* Teasing you? I'm not teasing you—these are pearls of wisdom coming from the mouth of your master. You should feel lucky to be so blessed.

JEN Bruce?

The other characters enter across the back as nightmare versions of themselves.

OTHERS *(singing)* We are Siamese if you please! We are Siamese if you don't please!

As BRUCE continues to beat her, the other characters also toss her around.

COREY What about your real dad?

EUGE Still ran out on you and your mom…

GRAM Broke her heart…

COREY If anyone is being racist, you are!

EUGE The illegitimate daughter.

GRAM Left her high and dry.

BRUCE What's wrong, Jen? Dragon got your tail?

JEN gets up and attacks them. The others fall away until she is only fighting BRUCE Lee.

JEN Okay you chicken shit Bruce Fucking Lee!!! You think I'm not good enough? You think I'm not worthy? You may be ashamed of me, but your blood runs through my veins. I flow with your power and the power of the universe!!! I don't care that you left! I'm just fine on my own!! I don't need you or anybody else!!!

JEN busts out and kicks the shit out of BRUCE. With a final burst of energy she tosses him down and pins him. Their eyes lock. She stops. The light dawns.

You're not my father.

BRUCE No, I am not.

JEN My father didn't leave me.

BRUCE No, he did not.

JEN My father loved me.

BRUCE Yes, yes he did.

JEN I miss him.

She begins to weep.

BRUCE Come, Little Dragon, it's all right to cry, but your father is still with you. Look into your soul. What do you see?

JEN Sadness and mourning.

BRUCE It is his sadness and mourning, that he is not with you.

JEN Confusion and doubt.

BRUCE What would your sensei say? *Tai sabaki*.... Stay grounded and keep moving...

BRUCE takes her by the hand and begins to engage in martial play with her.

"*Mo sut go sau*,"

JEN *(translating)* "The Grand Master of martial arts,"

BRUCE "*Ding teen lap day*,"

JEN "Standing tall as the sky, firm as the ground,"

BRUCE "*Yung gum cheen jun*,"

JEN "Courageously marching forward,"

BRUCE "*Fan bai wai sing*."

JEN "Turning defeat into victory."

BRUCE fades into the back. A ringing phone enters her consciousness. JEN slowly goes to answer it.

Hello...? Hey Mom...

Lights fade to black.

EPILOGUE

Spotlight on JEN centre stage, doing tai chi.

JEN I still don't know much about my real father. Mom's told me bits and pieces—how he loved *Star Trek*, how good he was at *gung fu*—it's still really hard for her to talk about him. Sometimes, I still think he's Bruce. Most times I don't. Whoever he is, I know he's in me. Somehow. In my blood, my veins. I can discover him by exploring the aspects of myself that never quite made sense—my stubborn single-mindedness, my pragmatic optimism. I define him by defining myself; I define myself by my relations with others, with the world. From each other. Through each other. All told, it starts to fill that void I'd never realized my father's absence had left in me. Bruce Lee describes a void as a form of process, ever-changing, full of potential. And—maybe because I'm Asian—I like that.

The other characters enter and together they bow. They begin to practise aikido with JEN. The movement continues—strong, sweeping, graceful, light; like big infinity symbols. Lights fade to black as the movement continues.

End.

THE UNFORGETTING

BY ALAN DILWORTH

ALAN DILWORTH

Alan Dilworth is a director, playwright, and teacher. He is co-artistic director of Sheep No Wool Theatre, and co-founder of Belltower Theatre. He is also the creator of Zero Hour, a theatre think lab investigating live performance. His directing credits include *The Unforgetting* (2004 SummerWorks Jury Prize), *If We Were Birds* (2008 SummerWorks Jury Prize), *The Gladstone Variations* (four Dora Mavor Moore Award nominations, including Production and Direction), and *Da* (Best Production at the Acting Irish International Theatre Festival). Alan was the 2005–06 Urjo Kareda Emerging Artist in Residence at Tarragon Theatre, and was named Toronto's Best Emerging Male Director for 2008 by *NOW Magazine*. Alan has an M.F.A. in directing from York University.

The Unforgetting was produced at the 2004 SummerWorks Theatre Festival by Belltower Theatre. I wrote and directed the play, but the entire process was a collaborative creation between the Belltower Theatre members: Maev Beaty, Patrick Robinson, and myself, and musical director and actor Andrew Penner. In the words of Anne Bogart, there were times when we worked with "fluidity between creative roles." Some days a section of text would fall flat and Patrick and Maev would find the words in rehearsal. Other days Andrew would be working with Maev and Patrick on a section of music and the staging or rhythm of a moment would become clear. This work was a struggle and a joy, and the piece managed to constantly surprise us. This production taught me that collaborating with amazing artists is a great privilege. This production taught me that collaborating with amazing artists is a great privilege, and is one of the reasons I love to collaborate as intensely and as often as I do.

Through the Lab Cab Festival's Artist Grant, created by the generous vision of Aviva Armour-Ostroff and André du Toit, and thanks to the hospitality of the Robinson family, Maev, Patrick, and I were able to rehearse a portion of the play at the Robinson family farm near Meaford, Ontario. The time we spent at the farm made an indelible mark on us and the work. The landscape and the horizon made its way into the poetry and rhythms of the play and its movement through theatrical time and space. Working in this environment was a remarkable opportunity.

The Unforgetting was well-received at the festival, and was given the SummerWorks Jury Prize that year. I was shocked and amazed at the response to the play. We had worked on this show very quietly, like we had created it in a black felt bag and had no idea what would come out. But when I think about who I was working with: Patrick, Maev, Andrew, lighting designer André du Toit, and costume designer Alison Chan, it is no surprise that the piece was well-received. They are extraordinary artists who gave so much of themselves and their work to the shaping of this play. It was one of the most exciting and rewarding creative journeys I have taken.

—Alan Dilworth

The Unforgetting was workshopped with Belltower Theatre co-founders Maev Beaty and Patrick Robinson. It was produced by Belltower Theatre at the 2004 SummerWorks Theatre Festival. The cast and crew of the SummerWorks production were:

PERCY Jenkins	Maev Beaty
DEVON Jenkins	Patrick Robinson
The RAILRIDER	Andrew Penner

Directed by Alan Dilworth
Lighting design by André du Toit
Costume design by Alison Chan
Stage managed by Steven Minnie
Music direction by Andrew Penner

Patrick Robinson and Maev Beaty; photo by Jim Van Meter.

On stage: there are eight logs, stool height. Two are upstage of centre, side by side ("the twin logs"), three run from downstage to upstage left, and three from downstage to upstage right.

The RAILRIDER sits on stage, scribbling in a sketchbook. We hear an incoming steam locomotive. The RAILRIDER, shabbily dressed, begins to sing a jubilant funeral hymn as he exits the stage. PERCY, wearing a clean, crisp linen dress, and DEVON, wearing a tie and vest, join in the hymn as they enter from opposite sides of the stage. As the hymn comes to a close, they stand facing the audience.

PERCY Fathers.

DEVON Funerals.

PERCY We all have one.

DEVON You have to have one.

PERCY Because we're all born.

DEVON We are all going to die.

PERCY Today was my father's funeral.

DEVON	The church was packed.
PERCY	It's no surprise.
DEVON	Every mayor in the Bulkley Valley paid their respects.
PERCY	Six ministers thronging the altar.
DEVON	Two women fainted.
PERCY	And no babies cried. A sign of their respect.
DEVON	Percy loves her father.
PERCY	Morgan Contractor, the most remarkable man I've ever known. My husband excepted.
DEVON	Rags to riches.
PERCY	A preacher, and a lumber pioneer.
DEVON	He was a…
BOTH	…very well-known man.

DEVON crosses to the twin logs.

DEVON	The day went off according to plan.
PERCY	It all happened so fast.
DEVON	Everyone closed their shops.
PERCY	Maybe we didn't do enough.
DEVON	It was the biggest funeral in Burns Lake history.

PERCY The premier sent his regrets.

DEVON He lives in Victoria.

PERCY The mill workers were poorly behaved.

DEVON Well, there's been a little trouble.

PERCY All that talking, where's their respect?

PERCY crosses to the twin logs.

DEVON Lumber prices have dropped.

PERCY My father worked harder than anyone, he created jobs for them.

DEVON Forty to twenty-five cents a day. They're calling it the Depression.

DEVON sits.

PERCY Rude is rude is rude.

DEVON Rude is rude is rude.

PERCY stands beside him, hands folded on his shoulder, we hear and see the flash of a camera. Beat. DEVON crosses downstage right and sits.

PERCY The guests have all gone home.

DEVON They are all eating dinner and talking about life as usual.

PERCY crosses to DEVON.

PERCY What are you saying?

DEVON I'm saying… I think many folks have a lot on their minds these days.

PERCY My father was a very important man.

DEVON Yes he was.

PERCY I don't appreciate your insinuation that folks have forgotten about him already.

DEVON I'm not saying they've forgotten your father. I am commenting on the situation that most folks find themselves in.

PERCY We seem to be getting along just fine.

DEVON Yes, well, we still have the mill, and the cost of living keeps dropping.

PERCY Not enough people appreciate what they have.

DEVON These days, not enough people have, period.

PERCY I am going to go through some of his letters. Could you clean some of the dishes?

DEVON I'll do the dishes. You get the letters from the front room.

PERCY Foyer.

DEVON Foyer.

DEVON turns on the radio.

RADIO VOICE Prime Minister Bennett threatens to take vote away from relief-camp workers.

PERCY ...Everything I smell, everything I hear, reminds me of Father.

RADIO VOICE Revelstoke mob beats man to death for stealing bread from the town mission.

PERCY It's the smell of his pipe, or seeing his cufflinks on his dresser.

RADIO VOICE More than a million unemployed—

PERCY I clean the hearth, and there are his spectacles.

RADIO VOICE Wages drop—

PERCY W.M.S. meeting, "We're so sorry about your father. What a man..."

RADIO VOICE Welfare lines—

PERCY I wash the floors, clean the kitchen, dust the office.

DEVON Sunday.

DEVON turns the radio off.

PERCY ...I wake up early and polish the silver he bought in Prince George...

DEVON Percy?

PERCY ...I clean the windows looking out on the cottage he built us for our wedding day.

DEVON Percy?

PERCY …I bake bread, sourdough… Daddy's favourite…

DEVON It's time to go to church.

They cross upstage and stand behind the twin logs.

PERCY The lord is my shepherd…

BOTH …I shall not want; he makes me lie down in green pastures, all the days of my life…. As it was in the beginning, it is now and ever shall be world without end. Amen.

DEVON "Let us pray for the soul of our brother Morgan Contractor."

BOTH Lord hear our prayer.

DEVON hands PERCY a handkerchief.

PERCY Thank you.

DEVON Lunchtime.

They cross downstage left.

PERCY Fresh snap peas…

DEVON Sliced tomatoes from the garden…

PERCY Roast beef…

DEVON Rhubarb pie. Bless us, oh Lord, for these thy…

There is a knock at the door.

Whoever it is must have smelt the food.

PERCY He crosses to the door.

DEVON A man.

PERCY A stranger.

BOTH A railrider.

DEVON Hello. How can I help you today?

RAILRIDER *(off)* I want to talk to him.

DEVON I'm sorry, I didn't hear you.

The RAILRIDER enters stage right.

RAILRIDER Where is he?

DEVON Pardon?

RAILRIDER Morgan Contractor.

DEVON Oh. I'm Morgan's son-in-law, Devon. This is Morgan's daughter, Percy. Would you like to come in? Please sit down, would you like some tea?

PERCY I'm sorry to have to tell you this, but my father passed away… just this past week.

DEVON I'm sorry…. I'm very sorry… if there's anything we can do…

The RAILRIDER exits. DEVON crosses to the door.

You're welcome to rest here for a time… and just like that he leaves.

PERCY You're welcome to rest here for a time?

DEVON Yes.

PERCY Tea?

DEVON I thought he looked like he could use some refreshment.

PERCY Darling, for all we know he was lying there snuggled up under the obituaries and saw Daddy's name. I didn't want him seeing the inside of the house.

DEVON Why not?

PERCY You have no sensibility of the home.

DEVON For all we know he could be the man who saved your father when he flipped his Ford.

PERCY For all we know he could be the man who burned the theatre in Prince George.

DEVON What are the chances?

PERCY What are the chances?

DEVON Let's just eat.

PERCY Fine. Let's eat.

They move downstage and sit opposite each other.

DEVON Roast beef?

PERCY No thank you. Tomatoes?

DEVON No thanks. Rhubarb pie?

PERCY To tell you the truth, I hate rhubarb pie.

DEVON You hate rhubarb pie?

PERCY I do. I despise rhubarb pie.

DEVON Then why do you always make it?

PERCY I make it for you.

DEVON Every Sunday you make rhubarb pie, hate it, and eat it, just for me?

PERCY Yes. Can we eat?

DEVON What else have you been doing just for me?

PERCY I don't want to talk about this anymore. Let's just eat.... Peas?

DEVON No thank you.

DEVON rises.

PERCY What's wrong now?

DEVON I've lost my appetite.

PERCY Why?

DEVON Because suddenly I'm afraid that you despise everything on your plate, but you're eating it all just for me.

PERCY You're being dramatic.

DEVON I'm going outside for a smoke, and you're not allowed to join me because I know you hate smoking.

DEVON exits.

PERCY Just so you know, I love blueberry pie, applesauce, chocolate cake, and ice cream… what I don't like are rhubarb pie, rice pudding with raisins, anything with raisins for that matter, oatmeal cookies with raisins, raisins with—

DEVON enters with a worn leather bag.

—that was a quick smoke.

DEVON This is the strangest thing.

PERCY I was telling you all the things I love and all the things I hate so you won't worry about me eating things I despise.

DEVON I owe you an apology.

PERCY Did I mention that I love apologies? Why do you owe me an apology?

DEVON Because I may have been wrong about letting that man into the house.

PERCY He took something.

DEVON No. He left something behind. *(crossing to PERCY)* I'm going to show this to you, but you have to remain calm.

PERCY Show me what it is.

DEVON Promise me you'll keep calm.

PERCY What is it?

DEVON Promise.

PERCY All right. I promise to keep calm.

DEVON pulls a revolver out of the bag.

Why does that man have a gun in his bag?

DEVON I don't know.

PERCY We're calling the police.

PERCY moves upstage right.

DEVON No. We are not calling the police.

PERCY A strange man with strange behaviour comes knocking on our door with a gun in his bag.

DEVON Lots of folks are carrying guns these days.

PERCY Yes, and the crazy ones should be locked up before they hurt somebody.

DEVON Your father carried one for a time.

PERCY	My father wasn't crazy.
DEVON	He did have a temper.
PERCY	My father had a backbone. Hello? Operator please. Yes, I'd like to speak with Captain O'Bannion. Thank you.... Captain, it's Percy Jenkins calling. I wanted to let you know that Dr. Jenkins and I had a very strange visitor today.... He looked like one. He didn't stay long, but he ended up leaving his bag behind, which had a gun in it.... Well very strange, and it made both the doctor and I very nervous.... No, you can't be too cautious these days. Well thank you very much.

DEVON puts on his hat.

DEVON	I can't believe you did that.
PERCY	It's for the good of the entire town. Where are you going?
DEVON	A man is about to beaten within an inch of his life.
PERCY	The captain will take care of things.
DEVON	That's why I am going, so I won't have to piece that man together later.
PERCY	Devon.

DEVON turns to exit.

DEVON	Her hands on her hips. She's beautiful.
PERCY	He turns and walks out the door.

DEVON I step out into the late-afternoon sun. "Dinner'll be sitting on the stove." From the house.

PERCY "I love you." From a distance.

DEVON moves downstage right. The twang of a slide guitar accents the text.

DEVON I am driving to town, I am looking for this man.... Over the covered bridge.... Stones and pebbles tickle the car.... Centre Street. Men in two's, men carrying guns.

PERCY ...putt, putt, putt, putt, putt, putt...

DEVON ...The shops are all empty, the shops are all closed.... Captain O'Bannion stands outside the station...

PERCY "Dr. Jenkins, what a surprise!"

DEVON No sign of him yet?

PERCY "Oh Doctor, we'll get him, I promise you that. I've called the whole town, we've got every man. Sixth Avenue is covered, and the twins are going to be looking by the tracks."

DEVON ...There's Wade and Wesley now, kicking a cat...

PERCY "Why don't you head on home, we're taking care of it for you here."

DEVON ...No sign along the river, no sign on Centre Street.... Ned!

PERCY "Hello, Devon. No sign of him yet. Someone saw

a fella walking out towards Ootsa, but it turned out to be a lumber boy. We'll get 'im."

DEVON Thanks, Ned. Spit arching out between his teeth. No sign at the tavern, or the hotel. No sign by the lumber yard or by the tracks... Maybe he left. Maybe he's trudging along the tracks on his way to a friendlier town.

PERCY moves upstage left.

PERCY The cupboard smells just like him. The silky weave of his preaching suit brushes my forearms, and I put my father's clothes on the bed. What else? Standing on the chair. Reaching up to the shelf, fingernails scraping something.... A metal box.... Oh. My father's prayer box from when he was a preacher... his Bible, bookmarked by a... deed. William Walker. His psalm book. "Morgan Contractor. 1894."..."Percy." He's home.

DEVON "I'll be right down." She's upstairs.

DEVON moves upstage and takes off his hat.

PERCY Box on the shelf, coming down the stairs. Any luck?

DEVON He's nowhere to be found.

PERCY Well maybe he's already left town.

DEVON Let's hope so.

PERCY Yes, let's hope so.

The telephone rings.

Hello, the Jenkins residence.... All right I'll tell him. Thank you.... The captain wanted you to know that Wade and Wesley think they spotted him over by the lumber yard.

DEVON The twins!

DEVON grabs the leather bag. During the following, PERCY and DEVON step side by side, one line at a time, downstage.

Feet hitting the floor, brown bag in hand.

PERCY Devon. He swings open the door.

DEVON Stepping across the porch floorboards, springing down the stairs.

PERCY Devon Jenkins. He's going towards the Ford.

DEVON She hikes up her dress and runs after me, feet massaging the gravel.

PERCY He gets to the car, turns the key, pulls the clutch.

DEVON Come on.

PERCY He gets to the car, turns the key, pulls the clutch.

DEVON Please.

PERCY My feet planted before the car.

DEVON Sputter, sputter. Thank you.

PERCY He looks up.

DEVON	I look up.
PERCY	"Get out of the way."
DEVON	She stands there.
PERCY	"Get out of the way."
DEVON	She doesn't budge. Percy, get out of the way.
PERCY	I step forward, knees rubbing the bumper. Where are you going with that gun?
DEVON	I am not going to let them tear this one apart.
PERCY	Get out of the car and give me the gun.
DEVON	No.
PERCY	I just lost my father, I'm not going to lose you.
DEVON	The engine coughs to a halt. Dammit. Percy steps up beside me.
PERCY	Give me the bag.
DEVON	I grab the bag.
PERCY	Give me the bag.
DEVON	Let go, Percy. My hand inside the bag.
PERCY	Just give it to me and let's be over with this.
DEVON	My hand is on the gun. Percy!
PERCY	Just give it.

DEVON Percy! The revolver unhooks from the bag.

PERCY Devon. The bag slides off his hand.

DEVON hands PERCY the RAILRIDER's sketchbook.

A black book falls open on the ground.

DEVON Do you realize that one of us could have been killed? What were you thinking?

PERCY Dear Lord.

DEVON The book lies open to a picture.

PERCY Impossible.

DEVON Flip.

PERCY He has a sketch of me in his book.

DEVON Flip.

PERCY My favourite dress, my doll I lost.

DEVON Flip.

PERCY This man drew me, this man knew me.

DEVON Flip.

PERCY At Miller's Rock, before the mill.

DEVON Flip.

PERCY My father, talking to a man.

DEVON Flip.

PERCY They're angry with each other, they're starting to quarrel.

DEVON Flip.

PERCY Quarrel turns tussle.

BOTH Flip.

DEVON Tussle turns close grips.

PERCY Flip.

DEVON Close grips turns throttling.

PERCY Flip.

DEVON Throttling turns grip of…

PERCY Oh!

PERCY buries her head in DEVON's chest.

DEVON Percy's father lays a thin man in the ground. Morgan Contractor… Morgan Contractor… again and again.

PERCY Are you finding this hard to believe?

DEVON Yes. You?

PERCY Yes. Very.

DEVON Why does he have these sketches?

PERCY I don't know.

DEVON No memories of any business like this?

PERCY No.

DEVON There's really no evidence to suggest that this really happened. The only things that are verifiable are that he somehow knew your father, Walker's Point, and you when you were a small child. I think we should avoid jumping to conclusions.

PERCY My father did not kill anybody.

DEVON Of course not.

PERCY It's absurd.

DEVON It is a little, isn't it.

PERCY It's insane.

DEVON I agree.

PERCY Give me the book.

DEVON Why?

PERCY Just give it to me.

PERCY grabs the book and turns to run inside.

DEVON Percy. She grabs the book and heads for the house.

PERCY Poker in hand, I open the stove.

DEVON I mount the steps, I go… Percy!

PERCY I burn the book.

DEVON I move for the stove, I burn my hand. Ow.

PERCY The book is gone.

DEVON An ash floats up between us.

PERCY The warm glow of flames on his face.

DEVON We need to discuss these things before you go ahead and do them.

The telephone rings. The telephone rings again. DEVON answers the phone.

Hello…? This is Dr. Jenkins…. Thank you for calling.

He hangs up.

There has been an accident. The man is dead.

Beat.

We have to go and find out if there is a body buried behind the mill.

PERCY What are you talking about?

DEVON Percy, there was a picture of your father laying a man in the ground.

PERCY You want to dig a hole in the ground to see if my father killed a man?

DEVON We only have a few hours of daylight left.

DEVON exits.

PERCY You want to— He turns and walks out the door.

DEVON enters with two shovels in hand.

DEVON One for you and one for me.

PERCY You think I'm going to dig?

DEVON crosses to upstage curtain.

DEVON Across the bridge. We know where the sketches say it happened.

PERCY crosses to upstage curtain.

PERCY Around the bend. Clouds moving in.

DEVON And behind the mill. Here we are.

PERCY Walker's Point.

BOTH Miller's Rock.

PERCY Devon standing, spade in hand.

DEVON It looks like rain. I guess we should get started.

PERCY Not a bird chirps, not a leaf flutters.

DEVON Shall we say a quick prayer?

PERCY Yes.

They pray.

Devon's spade rises up and hits the earth.

DEVON The grass is thick, you have to push hard.

PERCY The first clump of soil is dropped by the side.

DEVON This could take some time.

PERCY Spade after spade we dig into the ground. We work and we work until we're up to our knees.

DEVON How are your hands?

PERCY Fine. Yours?

DEVON Fine.

PERCY And we dig and we dig, until we're up to his waist.

DEVON So far, so good. According to those pictures it shouldn't be much deeper than this.

PERCY We should have found him by now.

DEVON Why don't you take a rest? And I dig and I dig.

PERCY And I take a rest.

DEVON Phew. I don't know. I think that's it.

PERCY And he wipes his brow.

DEVON So much for those pictures.

PERCY Amen.

DEVON Well—

PERCY And he stands his spade straight up in—

DEVON Crunch.

PERCY Devon? What is it?

DEVON Go get me a sheet from the house.

PERCY What is it?

DEVON Go get me a sheet.

PERCY This can't be true.

DEVON Percy, go!

PERCY exits.

Bone after bone uncovered in the dirt.

PERCY enters.

PERCY In through the front door and up the stairs. Cupboard door opens.... I move my father's prayer box off to the side. Pillowcase, pillowcase, old cotton sheet.... Across the bridge, around the bend, and behind the mill.... There must be some—

DEVON grabs the sheet from PERCY.

DEVON A perfect skeleton lies sleeping in the ground. We'll wrap them up and move them till we decide what to do.... Here, take this...

PERCY Did my father do this?

DEVON turns to leave, bundle of bones in his hand.

Where are we taking them?

DEVON The basement.

PERCY Our basement?

DEVON Beneath the stairs, where we keep the wood.

PERCY We can't.

DEVON Just until we decide what to do.

PERCY That was a living person.

DEVON Percy, it's just until we know what we're going to do. And we start off around the mill.

PERCY Rattle, rattle, rattle.

DEVON Around the bend.

PERCY Rattle, rattle, rattle.

DEVON Across the bridge.

PERCY Rattle, rattle, clunk.

DEVON Oh.

PERCY And Devon picks up the skull from the ground.

DEVON Sorry. Across the lawn and into the house. Down the hall and down the stairs.

DEVON exits stage right, bones in hand.

PERCY Behind the stairs and behind the wood.

DEVON re-enters, hands empty.

DEVON Up the stairs and into the light. Where's the key?

PERCY Key in my hand, key in the hole. Locked. Where are you going?

DEVON I need to think.

PERCY Devon. It had to have been some kind of mistake.

DEVON I'm sure it was.

PERCY And he turns and walks away.

DEVON gets into bed. He mumbles.

DEVON I'm sure it was. I'm sure it was.

PERCY gets into bed.

I'm sure it was. I'm sure it was.

PERCY Devon keeps sighing and talking in his sleep.

DEVON The bed keeps squeaking, she's been tossing and turning all night.

PERCY It's too hot tonight, the room has no air.

DEVON Bones in the basement, bones under stairs. Bones in my head when I close my eyes.

PERCY Squeak, creak. Devon sits up, trying to be quiet.

DEVON "Devon, what's wrong?" she says.

PERCY "Nothing, just having a little trouble falling asleep," he says.

DEVON "Would you open the window? It's stuffy in here."

PERCY "Of course. I'm just going to go downstairs and get a drink of water." His feet padding to the window.

DEVON "Thank you," from the bed. I tiptoe down the stairs.

DEVON crosses stage right.

PERCY I close my eyes and think about falling asleep.

DEVON Moonlight in the hall.

PERCY We bury the bones in a new place and forget this day ever happened.

DEVON stands, staring off stage right.

DEVON The door swings open, staring down the stairs, staring into black.

PERCY I am on Centre Street. The entire town is standing before me, facing a tall wooden platform. An aisle runs up the middle of the crowd and I walk up it. As I turn my head to the right… to the left… nobody looks at me. Their eyes are locked forward, waiting, waiting for something solemn… sacred. As I advance, I recognize them… Reverend Mueller, the Calvinist minister… Mary Cameron, the baker's wife… Walter Agum, the shoemaker.… I am standing before them, their eyes are trained on me. And they begin to move forward, forming a circle… which surrounds me.… A skirt brushes my leg… it tickles, a young hand grazes my shoulder. Mr. Price gives me a squeeze. Closer and closer. I am on the platform. Something scratchy and rough is placed around my neck.… I want to take it off, but my hands are pinned to my sides by the crowd pressing into me. The crowd is gone. No floor beneath me, rope wrapped around my neck, I look down into the cold, unfeeling eyes… of the Railrider.

The RAILRIDER, PERCY, and DEVON sing a haunting hymn in the round. PERCY crosses to stage left, where she burnt the book.

DEVON The morning.

PERCY A groggy morning. I want to have a service for the bones… you and I.

DEVON All right.

PERCY And then we can burn them in the furnace at the mill.

PERCY crosses stage left.

Over to the cupboard to find some words for a service.

DEVON Down the stairs where we keep the wood.

DEVON exits stage right.

PERCY Metal box from the shelf, a box full of prayers.

DEVON enters.

DEVON A bundle in my hand. Percy? Are you ready?

PERCY Down the stairs. Box in hand. Yes.

They cross to each other.

BOTH Over the bridge, around the bend, and into the mill.

PERCY Equipment everywhere.

DEVON crosses stage left.

DEVON Coal furnace. Steam engine.

PERCY Furnace gate open, Devon feeds it coal.

DEVON Not too much or it can be dangerous. But hot enough so they can burn.

PERCY Maybe you could read something appropriate.

DEVON crosses to PERCY.

DEVON Bible… psalm book…. What do you think of Lazarus?

PERCY I suppose.

DEVON I've never done this before.

PERCY No.

DEVON Gospel of John…

PERCY crosses stage right and puts down the box.

PERCY There may be a funeral service in one of them.

DEVON finds the deed tucked in the Bible.

DEVON William Walker…? This is a deed.

PERCY Maybe we could just say a few words.

DEVON Your father bought this land at auction.

PERCY What are you talking about, Devon?

DEVON Forfeited payments… abandonment clause…. Where was William Walker when your father bought this land…? Percy, what happened with your father wasn't a mistake.

PERCY How can you say that?

DEVON See for yourself. Everything we have—our house, your father's house, the mill—was built on this man's land.

PERCY takes the deed.

PERCY This is not our land. Dear Lord. My father took this man's land? My father was a murderer?

DEVON Percy…

PERCY He was a murderer, Devon, my God! How old was I? Where was I while he was digging that grave? Daddy.

DEVON crosses and comforts her. PERCY pulls away in order to leave.

We need to tell the police.

DEVON grabs her.

DEVON Okay, but let's just catch our breath.

PERCY Now.

DEVON Whoa, we need to think about this, Percy. This is a big discovery.

PERCY My father committed murder.

DEVON Yes, and your father is dead. What good will it do to go to the police?

PERCY This is stolen land.

DEVON Percy, Morgan's dead, William Walker is dead, even the man with the sketches is dead.

We can't change any of that. We burn the bones and we move on.

PERCY Move on?

DEVON We would lose the land. We would lose the mill. We would lose everything.

PERCY But Devon—

DEVON There's no work out there, Percy. People are hungry. There's no money. Our life is here.

PERCY pushes him away.

PERCY Please. Just take me home.

DEVON All right.

PERCY crosses downstage centre, followed by DEVON.

I'll be back. Across the bridge. Around the bend. And into the mill.... I burn the bones.

DEVON exits stage left. The RAILRIDER enters upstage right.

PERCY Devon? *(beat)* Devon? *(beat)* Devon...! I'm awake, I'm awake, I'm awake, I'm awake. I'm awake. I'm awake... I'M AWAKE!!

PERCY collapses and the RAILRIDER exits. DEVON enters stage left.

DEVON Percy. Percy. It's me. It's me. It's me. It's okay. It's okay. It's okay. It's okay.

PERCY regains her composure. They rise.

We're going to go see the captain.... We drive into town to see the captain.

PERCY We tell him about the bones.

DEVON And we tell him about the deed.

PERCY And just like that we lose our land.

DEVON Our mill.

PERCY And our home.

The RAILRIDER enters and crosses downstage right, singing a railroad song. DEVON exits. PERCY takes one last look at her home. DEVON returns with their suitcase. They cross downstage left and stand with their suitcase between them.

RAILRIDER I'm sorry, sir, this is first class, your wife and yourself will need to go down to the next car.

PERCY and DEVON cross to downstage right. The RAILRIDER crosses to stage left. The RAILRIDER, DEVON, and PERCY sing a verse of a railroad song together.

HOBO All aboard!

They sing the chorus of a railroad song. Curtain.

ANY NIGHT

BY DANIEL ARNOLD AND MEDINA HAHN

DualMinds

DualMinds is the creative team of Daniel Arnold and Medina Hahn. Their debut play *Tuesdays & Sundays* premiered at Theatre Network's NextFest in 2000, directed and dramaturged by Wojtek Kozlinski. *Tuesdays & Sundays* has since toured Canadian Fringes and professional theatres worldwide—including the National Arts Centre, the Edinburgh Festival, Prague, New Mexico, and New York—has garnered numerous awards, and has been listed among the "Best Plays of the Year" in Toronto, Edmonton, Vancouver, and New York. *Tuesdays & Sundays* was published twice, broadcast as a radio play on CBC and BBC, and has been optioned for a feature film. *Any Night* is DualMinds's second production. Arnold and Hahn were twice nominated as the Edmonton Mayor's Emerging Artists of the Year, have received ATP's Emerging Artist Scholarship, and for three years mentored with Daniel MacIvor. In 2008 MacIvor bestowed them with the protege portion of Canada's most prestigious theatre award: the Elinore and Lou Siminovitch Prize. They currently live in Vancouver, BC. For more information, visit www.dualminds.com.

DANIEL ARNOLD

Daniel is a professional actor and writer who graduated with a Bachelor of Fine Arts in acting from the University of Alberta in 2000. He has taken scriptwriting at the U of A, Workshop West, National Screen Institute, and under mentorship with Sharon Pollock. An actor since the age of twelve, Daniel continues to work professionally in theatre and on screen, writing for both mediums as well.

MEDINA HAHN

Medina is an actor, writer, and collaborator who has performed on numerous stages throughout the country and abroad. She comes to writing after working extensively as an actress on new plays—although she has kept a journal since she was nine. Medina's plays (co-written with Daniel Arnold) include: *Any Night*, *Clear Sunny Day*, and the multi-award winning *Tuesdays & Sundays*. She holds a Bachelor of Fine Arts in theatre from the University of Victoria and a Bachelor of Fine Arts in acting from the University of Alberta.

Any Night was born of two inspirations. The first was the tragic story of Ken Parks, a young married father in Scarborough, Ontario in 1987, who got up in the middle of the night, drove to his in-laws' house, almost beat his father-in-law to death with a tire iron, and then murdered his mother-in-law with a kitchen knife. It ended up being the first time in history that someone was found not guilty of murder because they were sleepwalking. The second inspiration came when we heard about a local family man who had installed hidden cameras to watch the university girl renting out his basement. We came up with the question: if someone was secretly being watched, would it affect their sleep? By extension we were asking: how powerful is our subconscious? The play then grew into a meditation on how and why we trust—or don't.

We performed and produced the original production ourselves, choosing the artists we wanted to work with, and designing the show to be remountable. We premiered *Any Night* in 2008, presented by Victoria's Belfry Theatre, then made some revisions before taking it to Toronto's SummerWorks Festival, which provided a great showcase for the work on a national scale.

The set for these productions consisted of a bed-like structure that could be lit from beneath, a pair of sheer curtains on a circular track (much like at a hospital), and a rolling three-step staircase with handrailings. These elements were moved and shifted in order to delineate different areas. The effect was to create a fluid and dreamlike state for Anna, never letting her know exactly where she was.

Props were either hidden under the bed or in the staircase steps (which were made into drawers). Neither actor ever left the stage, and Anna remained in pyjamas the entire time. Almost all Stranger and voice-over scenes used underscoring and even some live reverb.

That said, stage directions have been kept to a minimum to allow room for interpretation and imagination.

—Daniel Arnold & Medina Hahn

Any Night premiered in a production by DualMinds from February 26–March 1, 2008, presented by the Belfry Theatre (Victoria, BC) during their New Works Festival.

This production was then slightly revised and remounted by DualMinds from August 8–17, 2008, presented as part of the National Series of Toronto's SummerWorks Festival.

Produced by DualMinds (www.dualminds.com)

Director/dramaturge	Ron Jenkins
PATRICK/Playwright	Daniel Arnold
ANNA/Playwright	Medina Hahn
VOICEOVER	Brian Linds

Set/prop design by Peter Pokorny
Lighting design by David Fraser
Sound design by Gordon Heal
Costume design by Erin Macklem
Stage managed by Jennifer Swan

ACKNOWLEDGEMENTS

Any Night was originally commissioned by Theatre Network (Edmonton, AB), and received workshops or staged readings at Workshop West Theatre (Edmonton, AB), the Banff Playwrights Colony (a collaboration between Alberta Theatre Projects, the Banff Centre for the Arts, and the Canada Council for the Arts), and the Magic Theatre (San Francisco, CA). *Any Night* was also made possible through the generous support of Vancouver's Playhouse Theatre Company and the Spirit of BC Commissioning Program.

The creation, premiere, and touring of *Any Night* would not have been possible without the support of the BC Arts Council and the Canada Council for the Arts.

The playwrights also wish to thank Bradley Moss, Wojtek Kozlinski, Antje Oegel, Glynis Leyshon, Chelsea McPeake, Andy Thompson, Jamie Nesbitt, Paul Moniz de Sa, Matthew Payne, Western Canada Express, Corinne Kessel, Greenscape Silk Designs, Jessica Heidt, Ron Shetler and the Shetler Studios, David Nugent, Erin Moon, Matthew Edison, Ian Leung, Jamie Konchak, Elinor Holt, Roy Surette, Michael Rubenfeld and the staff of the 2008 SummerWorks Theatre Festival, Michael Shamata and the staff at the Belfry Theatre, the University of Alberta Hospital, Sleep Psychologist Jonathan Fleming, and give special thanks to our families for their unconditional support, Daniel MacIvor for taking us in, Ron Jenkins for the constant collaboration, and to the late June Callwood.

CHARACTERS

ANNA, 20s
PATRICK, 20s

PATRICK also plays:
THE STRANGER
BEN, 20s—Anna's ex
COLETTE, 30s—the neighbour, a psychic with an accent
MADDIE, 80s—the landlady

There are also recorded voices:
PATRICK in the past
PETE, a sleep-lab technician

SETTING

Limbo

TIME

Now

Daniel Arnold and Medina Hahn; photo by Stephanie Hull.

SCENE ONE

A bed.

Sounds of a car. A fire.

Shattering glass, then silence.

STRANGER Are you with me?

ANNA One of us is dead

STRANGER Are you with me?

ANNA One of us is dead

And one of us has died inside

But I can't tell which

STRANGER Why do you say that?

ANNA We live our lives forward, but we only understand them backward

STRANGER Okay.

ANNA I was looking for a place to live

STRANGER Okay.

ANNA I saw a sign:

"Bright, spacious basement suite"

"View Any Night between 7 and 9"

STRANGER Okay, stay with me.

ANNA One of us will die, and one of us will die inside

STRANGER It'll be all right.

ANNA But I can't tell which

STRANGER I'm right here, trust me. No one will die.

ANNA Patrick

STRANGER Just trust me.

ANNA Patrick

STRANGER Who?

ANNA Patrick!

STRANGER I'm not Patrick.

Shift.

SCENE TWO

ANNA stands outside the door. Patrick stands inside.

PATRICK ...Hi.

ANNA Hi...

Sorry, I'm here about the basement suite?

PATRICK Oh. Yeah. I'm not the landlady. Obviously. She's not in right now.

ANNA Oh.

PATRICK But I can show you around if you want.

ANNA Sure.

PATRICK Come on in.

She does.

That's a nice looking sweater.

She's barefoot and wearing pyjamas.

ANNA ...Thanks.

You live up here?

PATRICK Yuh, just down the hall. And this would be yours down here. Right below me. If you wanna take it.

Light spills in.

ANNA Oh…

PATRICK Yeah, lots of light for a basement, hey?

ANNA It's lovely.

PATRICK Yeah.

ANNA It doesn't even feel like a basement.

PATRICK I know.

ANNA Why's it so cheap?

PATRICK Don't really know. Maddie, the landlady, she's getting old, hasn't raised the rent in like ten years.

ANNA Huh.

PATRICK Oh, but she lives up in the loft, and she's pretty serious about it being a no pets, no smoking thing…

ANNA Oh, that's good, I'm trying to quit.

PATRICK Perfect.

ANNA And it's available right now?

PATRICK Yeah, last person moved out mid-month. Bit of a wackjob.

ANNA looks at him.

Crazy.

Is it just for yourself or…?

ANNA Yeah.

PATRICK How'd you find out about it?

ANNA There was a notice up at my dance studio.

PATRICK Oh yeah, I probably put that up. Cool, you dance?

ANNA Yeah. And teach, choreograph, waitress…

PATRICK Right. Cool. I took breakdancing when I was a kid. *(pulls a breakdancing move)* Always wish I kept it up, you know?

ANNA Oh yeah?

PATRICK …I'm Patrick, by the way.

ANNA Hi. Anna.

PATRICK Anna, hi.

They shake hands. The moment is suspended.

ANNA Have we met before?

PATRICK No, I don't think so. I think I'd remember meeting you.

Can I have my hand back?

ANNA Sorry…

PATRICK So…?

ANNA I'll take it.

SCENE THREE

Sounds of a lab, monitored breathing, heart rate, a steady beeping. ANNA*'s lying in bed, asleep.* PATRICK *has disappeared.*

A *voice-over conversation plays to the lazy sounds of a card game:*

PATRICK *(voice-over)* What's wrong with her?

PETE *(voice-over)* Don't know. They don't tell me nothin'.

PATRICK *(voice-over)* Yeah, right.

PETE *(voice-over)* Hey, my deal.

A *pause while the cards are shuffled.*

PATRICK *(voice-over)* She's cute.

PETE *(voice-over)* Get away from there.

PATRICK *(voice-over)* What? I'm just looking.

PETE *(voice-over)* Come on, you're not even supposed to be here.

ANNA *sits up.*

PATRICK *(voice-over)* Oh.

PETE *(voice-over)* What?

PATRICK *(voice-over)* She's moving.

PETE *(voice-over)* Ah crap, lie down, honey. I'm trying to play cards.

ANNA *stares.*

PATRICK *(voice-over)* Oh shit, is she looking at us?

PETE *(voice-over)* She can't see us. She's asleep. Besides it's a two-way mirror.

ANNA *walks towards them.*

PATRICK *(voice-over)* Can she hear us?

PETE *(voice-over)* Soundproof walls. Come on, ante up.

SCENE FOUR

Lightning, thunder, heavy rain.

ANNA *is now carrying a box.*

PATRICK Hey!

ANNA Hi—this is slipping, one second!

PATRICK What, are you moving in right now?

ANNA One second, one second!

PATRICK In the middle of a storm?

ANNA Agh, one second! Is it ever coming down!

PATRICK Totally yeah, cats and dogs.

Need a hand?

ANNA Please. My stuff is getting drenched!

Blackout.

Beat.

Did the power go out?

PATRICK No, my shoulder hit the light switch, sorry.

ANNA Oh, well can you turn it back on?

PATRICK Yuh, I just can't find it.

ANNA This stuff is slipping, so um…

PATRICK Just put it down.

ANNA I can't, something's…

PATRICK God, where's the stupid switch?

ANNA Can you hurry please?

PATRICK Hold your horses!

ANNA Ah, shit.

A crash. Beat.

PATRICK Found it.

The light turns on. They're in her room, a wet box lies at ANNA's feet.

ANNA Hold your horses? Who says that?

PATRICK I grew up on a farm. Sorry.

ANNA *pulls out an alarm clock, which is broken.*

ANNA Ah, shit.

PATRICK Oh no, sorry. Now you'll *never* wake up.

Sorry about that, I'll get you a new one.

ANNA It's okay.

PATRICK No, I think I have an extra one. I'll totally give it to you.

He looks downstage.

Hey, cool mirror.

He goes downstage into the light of a full-length mirror.

Is it broken or supposed to be like that?

ANNA Supposed to be like that.

PATRICK Mirror in the shape of a sliver moon.

He traces his finger along the edge of the glass.

You're really hot.

ANNA What?

PATRICK Oh, nothing, just… telling myself I was hot. Never mind. Aw, is that you?

ANNA *has a picture frame.*

ANNA Yeah, always wanted to be a ballerina.

PATRICK Aw, and now you are.

ANNA Well…

PATRICK Well, what kind of dance do you do?

ANNA Mostly modern.

PATRICK Oh. Still, you're living the dream. *(about the picture)* So cute.

ANNA Hey, thanks for helping me.

She goes to hang the frame.

PATRICK Sure— Oh, I wouldn't put that there. Sometimes when it rains it leaks a bit.

ANNA Oh.

PATRICK Same with the corner, gets kind of damp. Sorry, did I forget to mention that? It's no big deal. I just wouldn't hang anything nice there.

ANNA Okay.

PATRICK Other than that, the place okay so far?

ANNA Yeah, just wish I could just snap my fingers and it would all be clean.

PATRICK Uh, I cleaned when they moved out, is it not…

ANNA Oh, no, I just mean all my stuff.

PATRICK Oh yeah, I hear ya.

ANNA And I should get some curtains for this window—

In a strike of lightning, a shadow passes by the window.

Oh! God…

PATRICK What?

ANNA *(looking out)* Oh my God…

PATRICK What? What is it?

ANNA Ben.

PATRICK Who?

ANNA My… ex.

PATRICK Are you expecting him?

ANNA No. I never told him where I was. Fuck.

Fuck, fuck, fuck. Sorry, I'm gonna have to deal with this.

PATRICK Yeah, of course.

SCENE FIVE

PATRICK is now silhouetted (as BEN).

ANNA — No! BEN— LET GO! I DON'T WANT TO TALK TO YOU, I DON'T WANT TO HEAR FROM YOU—

BEN — You're being dramatic.

ANNA — No more fucking *lies*.

BEN — What— I haven't lied!

ANNA — You're following me.

BEN — What?

ANNA — How did you find me?

Beat.

How did you find me!

BEN — You know, I'm not just some piece of shit you can walk out on without a word.

ANNA — I told you I was / leaving—

BEN — Your stuff was gone when I got home!

ANNA — Look. You've been following me, you've been watching me—

BEN — What? This is crazy.

ANNA Listening to my phone messages, showing up at my studio—

BEN Yeah, cuz you're acting crazy! Getting up and leaving in the middle of the night. Is there someone else?

ANNA No. How did you find me?

BEN I asked at your studio! I'm not following you! Where is this coming from? Is this your dream shit again?

ANNA I'm dying, okay? I'm suffocating. I need to be alone. I've tried to tell you that. I need to be alone. And the tighter you hold, the farther I'll push. It's done.

She takes off her engagement ring.

BEN So that's it?

ANNA Yeah, that's it.

BEN takes the ring and disappears. Shift.

SCENE SIX

ANNA shivers. The STRANGER is there.

ANNA I'm dying

I'm suffocating

STRANGER Shhh…

ANNA — I need to be alone

I've tried to tell you that

Beat.

I'm so thirsty

SCENE SEVEN

Knock, knock, knock.

PATRICK — It's Patrick.

ANNA — Come in.

He does.

PATRICK — Thirsty? *(beat)* Brought you some wine.

ANNA — Oh. Thanks.

PATRICK — Thought you might need it.

ANNA — Sorry, could you hear?

PATRICK — No, not really. *(beat)* Yes.

You okay?

ANNA — Yeah.

PATRICK — You moved out without telling him?

ANNA — Uh…

PATRICK Harsh.

ANNA No, I told him, he just didn't want to hear it.

PATRICK I make it myself, in the garage—what do you think?

ANNA Not bad.

PATRICK "Not bad"?

ANNA It's good.

PATRICK Well, gets better the more you have.

She smiles. He hands her an alarm clock.

ANNA Oh, thank you. You didn't have to.

PATRICK Yes I did. It's an old one, used to go off all the time, but I think I fixed it.

ANNA Okay.

He's got a glass too, and they both sip.

PATRICK You sure you're okay?

ANNA Yeah, I'm fine, just need to sleep.

PATRICK You need some curtains for your windows tonight?

ANNA It's all right, I'll deal with it tomorrow.

PATRICK Okay. Okay well, I take care of the house for Maddie, so… you ever need anything, you know where to find me.

ANNA Yeah.

PATRICK Okay, well. Sleep well. Welcome to the neighbourhood.

ANNA Thanks.

Shift.

SCENE EIGHT

She looks around, shivering again. The STRANGER is in the distance.

ANNA …there's glass everywhere…

Sound of a speeding car as she crawls into bed.

Glass shatters.

SCENE NINE

ANNA *sits up.* PATRICK*'s outside her broken window.*

ANNA Oh God!

PATRICK Sorry.

ANNA What are you doing?

PATRICK Nothing, sorry—

ANNA What are you doing?

PATRICK Nothing, nothing, just waiting for you to wake up.

ANNA What? Why?

PATRICK You don't remember?

ANNA Remember what?

PATRICK Oh my God, I thought you'd remember. I came down last night cuz I heard you scream.

ANNA What?

PATRICK Yeah. At like three o'clock. I heard this scream and breaking glass. You don't remember a thing?

ANNA *looks around, disoriented.*

Man… I came down to your door, you know, to see what was wrong, and I could hear you choking, like crying and choking. I knocked on the door but there was no answer. I thought maybe your ex had come back.

ANNA What?

PATRICK Yeah, so I ran outside and was calling the cops just in case, but then I saw you just kneeling in bed. Sort of hugging yourself, and rocking yourself, and no one was there. Your window was smashed but no one was there.

After a bit, you just lay back down. Haven't moved till now.

She takes a moment to absorb this.

ANNA You stayed out there?

PATRICK Yeah, I was worried about you.

ANNA You watched me?

PATRICK What? No, I just sat with my back to the window, to keep the cold out of your room.

ANNA *looks around.*

You don't remember a thing?

She looks down at her hands.

Are they okay?

ANNA They're fine.

He picks some glass from the window.

PATRICK Well, I know what I'm doing the rest of the morning.

You gonna be okay?

She walks down to her sliver-moon mirror, the lights fading around her…

Anna, you okay?

She leans forward, looking intently at herself.

Anna? You gonna be okay…?

She breathes out on the glass.

SCENE TEN

A tarot card drops from the heavens.

ANNA *looks at it, picks it up, and stares at it.*

SCENE ELEVEN

ANNA *stares at the card in her hand. She's now in the backyard.* PATRICK*'s on the porch, smoking, listening to his iPod.*

PATRICK Hey. What's that?

ANNA A tarot card…

I found it on the sidewalk.

PATRICK Oh. Probably Colette's. The lady next door. She claims to be psychic.

ANNA *(handing it to him)* It's the Death card.

PATRICK Shit, well don't give it to me!

ANNA Could just mean change. Depends on the way it's dealt.

PATRICK What, you read them?

ANNA I go sometimes.

PATRICK No—to her?

ANNA No. But now I guess I have to.

PATRICK snickers.

What, you don't believe people can see things before they happen?

PATRICK Sure sure, just don't know if she's the one to be seeing it.

ANNA Why not?

PATRICK Colette? I don't see psychic coming from her. Plays the part a bit too much.

ANNA Have you gone?

PATRICK No.

ANNA Then how can you say?

PATRICK Cuz she's always leaning over the fence telling me I'm gonna die.

He smiles.

ANNA I thought it was non-smoking.

PATRICK Not *outside*.

ANNA Can I have a drag?

PATRICK Thought you were quitting.

ANNA Not *outside*.

She sits down next to him.

What are you listening to?

He gives her a headphone.

Burial? Are you kidding? I love him!

PATRICK No, really? I didn't think anyone else knew him.

ANNA They don't. He hasn't hit mainstream.

PATRICK I know.

ANNA I'm actually using one of his songs for the new solo I'm working on.

PATRICK Cool, which one?

ANNA "Tortured."

PATRICK Nice. Me too. I'm working on a solo.

ANNA Really?

PATRICK Yuh—it's called "Robot."

He robot dances.

ANNA Smartass.

They smile.

Hey so listen, about last night. Do you know if Maddie heard?

PATRICK Haven't talked to her. But she takes her hearing aids out at night, so…

ANNA Oh, perfect. 'Kay, can we just keep that between you and I then? I don't really want her to think she's got a freak living in the basement.

PATRICK Okay.

ANNA Sorry if I scared you.

PATRICK You sure your ex didn't come back?

ANNA Ben? Doubt it. It was probably me. New environments can throw me off.

PATRICK What, what do you mean?

ANNA Last time I stayed in a hotel, I woke up on the balcony. They found me dropping miniature soaps on people's heads.

PATRICK Hilarious. You sleepwalk?

ANNA Yeah, been to a specialist; even spent some time in a sleep lab.

PATRICK Sleep lab, what's that?

ANNA Uhh… they hook you up to all these machines and monitor your sleep. With cameras and everything.

PATRICK God, what was that like?

ANNA Stressful. Gave me nightmares.

PATRICK I can imagine.

ANNA But don't worry, I went to the doctor and I'm taking some pills, so… I'm not gonna kill you in your sleep.

PATRICK Thanks.

ANNA Anyway, sorry about the window.

PATRICK No, no, don't worry about it. I found a storm window in the garage, replaced it with that. And I put up curtains, cleaned. Everything's fine.

ANNA What?

PATRICK Yeah.

ANNA Wait, sorry, you cleaned my place?

PATRICK Yeah. Well, there was glass all over. And you said you wanted to just snap your fingers and it would all be clean, so…

ANNA How'd you get in?

PATRICK My key.

ANNA What?

PATRICK I'm the caretaker, so…

ANNA That's a complete invasion of privacy. I never asked you to do that. You can't just come into my place whenever you want. You had no right to do that.

PATRICK Sorry, sorry, I just…. Okay, you're right, that wasn't okay. I shouldn't have done that. I'm totally sorry. It'll never happen again.

ANNA Good.

PATRICK I hope this doesn't… make things weird. You just said you needed curtains, you said the place wasn't clean. I wanted to do something nice. Seemed you could, you know, use something nice.

Shift…

SCENE TWELVE

She's back with the STRANGER.

ANNA I changed my locks

That night

I changed my locks

SCENE THIRTEEN

The sounds of the sleep lab creep back in. ANNA, *alone, begins to dance in her sleep. Voices over the speakers again:*

PATRICK *(voice-over)* Is she dancing?

PETE *(voice-over)* Kinda looks like it, doesn't it?

PATRICK *(voice-over)* That's fucking freaky.

PETE *(voice-over)* Yeah. Every night so far. Gets up, wanders around, dances.

PATRICK *(voice-over)* What the hell's wrong with her?

PETE *(voice-over)* I think it's a confusional arousal.

PATRICK *(voice-over)* Arousal? Pete, I'm no doctor, but that sounds hot.

PETE *(voice-over)* No, a night terror, it's like… acting out a nightmare, but you're still asleep. Like sleep-walking through a nightmare. Kind of.

Hell, don't ask me, I just get paid to watch.

Beat. They watch her.

PATRICK *(voice-over)* Does she say anything?

PETE *(voice-over)* Calls out for her mother sometimes.

PATRICK *(voice-over)* God, look at her eyes…

PETE *(voice-over)* Scary, isn't it?

PATRICK *(voice-over)* And these are her brainwaves?

PETE *(voice-over)* Yup.

PATRICK *(voice-over)* Look at them. It looks like an earth-quake. And she's totally asleep?

PETE *(voice-over)* Yup. All normal when you sleepwalk.

PATRICK *(voice-over)* Pete, you know what you could do?

PETE *(voice-over)* What?

PATRICK *(voice-over)* You could sell tickets to this.

PETE *(voice-over)* What?

PATRICK *(voice-over)* Yeah, set up some seats in here, charge people to come in, you'd make a killing.

PETE *(voice-over)* Jesus.

PATRICK *(voice-over)* Hey, get 'er topless, you could take her to Vegas.

PETE *(voice-over)* That's it, go get me a coffee.

SCENE FOURTEEN

A phone starts ringng. ANNA *is now in bed. She suddenly sits up.*

ANNA Hello?

Hello…?

Ben?

A dial tone.

After a moment, she looks up at the ceiling. PATRICK *is in his room, typing on his computer.*

Patrick…?

Patrick?

Patrick!

He looks down to the floor.

PATRICK Yeah?

ANNA You can hear me?

PATRICK Well, when you yell right up into the vent, yeah I guess. Why, what's up?

ANNA I want to say sorry.

PATRICK Okay.

ANNA For the other day. For getting mad like that.

PATRICK Okay.

ANNA I know you were just trying to be nice.

PATRICK Okay.

ANNA Okay?

PATRICK Okay.

Shift.

SCENE FIFTEEN

The sound of a car crash.

ANNA *bolts up.*

She walks out of her room and up to PATRICK*'s door.*

PATRICK Anna?

She shakes his door.

Anna?

PATRICK opens his door.

Anna…?

She breathes out on his face, and reaches out to him.

Anna.

He grabs her hand.

SCENE SIXTEEN

She wakes in PATRICK's room; he's holding her hand.

ANNA Oh. Sorry.

PATRICK What's the matter? You're not gonna kill me, are ya?

ANNA I don't think so.

PATRICK Great.

You okay? You… awake?

ANNA Yeah.

PATRICK You wanna come in, or…?

ANNA I think Ben keeps calling.

PATRICK Jesus, really? Are you okay?

ANNA He's probably just drunk.

Nice room.

PATRICK Ha. This old thing?

ANNA What's with the bars on the window?

PATRICK Oh, just got a lot of expensive equipment.

ANNA That might be a good idea for my place. Don't go doing it or anything—just thinking out loud.

What is all this stuff?

PATRICK Oh, you know, tech-dweeb things. Mostly for work.

ANNA What do you do?

PATRICK Design, some editing, some content creation. Basically contract work for a few NGOs.

ANNA NG-whos?

PATRICK Oh. Amnesty, Unicef, things like that?

ANNA Wow. Really?

PATRICK Yeah. Doing this site right now for World Without Borders, you heard of it?

ANNA No.

PATRICK Cool mandate, actually. Basically, take down all the borders, anyone can go wherever they want, at any time. No passports, no visas, like no divisions at all.

ANNA Sounds like chaos.

PATRICK You think?

ANNA It's a beautiful idea though. A world without walls.

PATRICK Yeah. And it's paying me, so…

Oh my God, I should show you! You got a minute?

ANNA Yeah, can't sleep anyway…

PATRICK 'Kay, there's this program—I did motion capture for a while and I stole this hardware… here, give me your hand.

He sticks an electrode to her, which is attached to his computer. He clicks his mouse a few times, then takes her hand and moves it up and down. Her movement shows up on his computer screen.

Neat, hey?

ANNA Yeah.

PATRICK They use it a lot for videogaming and animation, but I just kinda stole it cuz I think it's cool.

She dances with her hand.

And what a way to choreograph a dance, hey? Cuz there's a whole set, you can put them all over your body. So just think, you could dance it once when you're all hooked up, then it's recorded. You could send it to your dancers, just like that, or change the order, stretch a moment out, repeat a bit—anything you want. And it's all laid out for you, right on the screen.

ANNA Weird.

PATRICK Weird?

ANNA Yeah, that it can be so technical. It's like dating over the Internet, you don't have to do the real thing.

PATRICK Ha, no, you just don't understand it.

ANNA No, I do. But I'd rather not. I'd rather the work, the sweat. I'd rather fall in love and not completely understand—you know?

PATRICK Okay.

Hey, can I ask you…? You know that morning, when you broke your window… what was that thing you did with your mirror? Did you breathe on it, or… what was that?

ANNA Oh. Yeah. Sometimes when I sleepwalk, I can tell I'm doing it. But I still can't wake myself up, you know? But I figured out if I find a mirror, and I breathe on it… somehow when I see my breath in front of my face, it wakes me up. Like a real sign I'm alive. Awake.

I know, I'm weird.

PATRICK Cuz you just did that to me.

ANNA Really?

He breathes out on her face.

Shift.

SCENE SEVENTEEN

She starts to gasp for breath. The STRANGER is there again.

ANNA I'm cold

Where am I?

There's stars on the ground

She watches the STRANGER for a moment.

You have a very kind face

What's your name?

SCENE EIGHTEEN

PATRICK appears silhouetted (as COLETTE).

COLETTE I am Colette.

Thank you for bringing my card back.

ANNA Of course.

COLETTE I left it for you, you know.

ANNA Really?

COLETTE Mm-hmmmm.

ANNA The Death card?

COLETTE Could just mean change. Depends the way it's dealt. Would you like some tea?

ANNA I'm good, thanks.

COLETTE Are you sure? It's Sleepy Time.

Shuffle.

She hands ANNA *the cards, who starts shuffling.* COLETTE *hums, loudly.*

ANNA I'm done.

COLETTE Mn, good, now: pick a card.

She does.

Mm, the Lovers.

One of you will die. And one of you will die inside.

ANNA What?

COLETTE I said one of you will die inside; and one of you will die.

ANNA What?

COLETTE Die.

Die inside…

And die.

ANNA *flicks all the cards.*

SCENE NINETEEN

The cards fly everywhere.

PATRICK Agh! Anna! It's not fifty-two pickup!

They're down in her room.

ANNA That's what I wanted to do!

PATRICK What, to her face?

ANNA Yeah, she was so weird!

PATRICK Told you. Why, what'd she say?

ANNA She was all, "One of you will die, and one of you will die—inside!"

PATRICK I told you, she's a total nutbar.

ANNA Well, at least it was free.

They pick up the cards.

It's good you're here.

PATRICK Huh?

ANNA Most of my friends are kind of Ben's friends too, so… it's good you're here. You're a good distraction.

PATRICK Distraction, thanks.

ANNA You know what I mean. I like you. You're nice to hang out with. You calm me down.

PATRICK Yeah, I think that's cuz I'm boring. "Do you wanna play cards?" What am I thinking?

ANNA Isn't that a good sign? When you can just hang out and do nothing with someone and still have fun?

PATRICK Yeah, you know what—it is.

ANNA *knocks.*

What the hell, you're knocking already?

ANNA I got a good hand.

What do you got?

PATRICK I don't know—jack shit, obviously.

ANNA Thirty and a half.

PATRICK I *dealt* you three aces?

ANNA Pure skill.

PATRICK laughs.

Pure, unbridled skill.

A moment.

PATRICK Do you wanna go somewhere? I wanna go somewhere. Do you wanna like… go somewhere? Have *fun* somewhere? Do you wanna, like… go out somewhere?

ANNA Where?

PATRICK I don't know. Like dinner, or dancing, or whatever people do?

ANNA Dancing?

PATRICK No, you're right, fuck dancing, but like food, people, fun, somewhere? I know this great Greek restaurant—

ANNA I love Greek. It's my favourite.

PATRICK Really? Perfect. Perfect—I know this little place right outside the city. Great people, amazing view, breaking plates. You in?

ANNA Sure.

PATRICK Like, right now?

ANNA Why not?

PATRICK You're serious.

ANNA Yes, before I change my mind.

PATRICK No, no. Yeah, okay. Wicked, it's a date.

SCENE TWENTY

The song "Sweet Dreams" by the Eurythmics starts playing. PATRICK and ANNA do a lip-synch performance to the song.

When they finish, they return to the table.

PATRICK Yeah! That was awful!

ANNA You didn't warn me it was lip-synch night!

PATRICK I didn't know! I'm so sorry, I haven't been here in forever, it's totally changed.

ANNA It's like a drag show for straight people.

PATRICK You know, you got a great set of pipes.

ANNA Thanks.

PATRICK Man, do these Greeks know how to party or what? Opa!

Another song has started, a slower one that someone else is performing, badly…

ANNA Oh, God…

PATRICK …Let's dance.

PATRICK takes her, and they slow dance.

So what would your dream night be?

ANNA What?

PATRICK Like the *best* night of your life? What would it be?

ANNA What do you mean?

PATRICK What would you be doing? Don't think about it. Just picture it: the first image that comes to your mind—

ANNA Uh—

PATRICK Don't think, just one image—the best night of your life, what are you doing?

ANNA Um, the final pose of my solo show, I'm at the Joyce, it's sold out—

PATRICK Joyce?

ANNA Joyce. Theatre, New York, famous.

PATRICK Okay.

ANNA This is so self-indulgent.

PATRICK It's okay, whatever. Dream night.

ANNA Okay. My final pose, everyone's standing, I can see the first few rows of people, and tears are coming down their faces.

PATRICK Aw. Okay, and then… what then? Everyone's cheering, standing ovation, sold out at the Joyce, then what? It's the *best* night of your life, you get off stage and what next?

ANNA Uh…

PATRICK Don't think about it!

ANNA Uh, there's a huge party—

PATRICK Okay.

ANNA Everyone's there, big-time producers, Isadora Duncan's there—

PATRICK Who's this?

ANNA Oh my God, most famous dancer ever. She *made* modern dance, tore through her life, lovers, she's dead now—

PATRICK Oh.

ANNA Yeah, died in a car when her scarf—one of those long-flowing scarves—got wrapped around the spokes of the back tire, this is like 1927—and she was yanked right out—

PATRICK Oh my God.

ANNA I know.

PATRICK Okay, no, happy happy, *best* night of your life, best night, no one's dying—

ANNA Right, okay, well anyway, Isadora Duncan's there, in spirit anyways, maybe Martha Graham's there in spirit—

PATRICK Who's this?

ANNA Martha Graham?!

PATRICK Famous dancer. Okay, all the famous dancers are there, in spirit, alive, whatever.

ANNA Yeah, and my mom's there, my family, my friends—

PATRICK Okay, yeah, champagne, you're the toast of the town, the country, the world—and then what?

ANNA Then… I don't know, Robert Rodriguez walks in.

PATRICK Robert Rodriguez? The filmmaker?

ANNA Yeah.

PATRICK Robert Rodriguez.

ANNA Yeah, he introduces himself and says he was so moved that he *needs* to create a role for me in his next movie—a silent one, of course. Ah! And it's opposite Johnny Depp!

PATRICK Oh my God.

ANNA And then Johnny steps out from the shadows! Says he loved my show.

PATRICK Okay, okay, so you go home with both of them.

ANNA No, no, we go out, a bunch of us, Robert, Johnny, all my close friends, we go out to some private club—

PATRICK Greek food?

ANNA Yeah, Greek food—and lip-synching! And there's probably drugs, like peyote, or something I've never tried, and we just have a blast, you know, get to know each other—

PATRICK Jesus— Okay, and then?

ANNA Then, uh, I go home, you know—

PATRICK But Johnny Depp comes.

ANNA No, I turn him down, him *and* Robert, I'm already in love.

PATRICK What? With who?

ANNA My boyfriend.

PATRICK You turn down Johnny Depp to stay with your frickin' boyfriend?

ANNA It's a match made in heaven, it's blissful love, has been for years.

PATRICK Okay, okay, so you go home with your boyfriend, who's *not* Johnny Depp, and where do you live?

ANNA Uh, one of those big lofts in New York, where I have a studio in my own place—oh my God—I come home, my boyfriend pays the babysitter, and then we go to bed.

PATRICK And make love, hopefully.

ANNA Of course. And then we fall asleep in each other's arms.

PATRICK And how do you sleep?

ANNA Like a baby.

PATRICK Any dreams?

ANNA Nothing. Then in the morning… I wake up, the sun's pouring in, I go look outside, and my boyfriend and our kids are having a car wash, and I think… that was the best night of my life.

Beat.

PATRICK Okay.

Okay.

ANNA What's yours?

PATRICK Oh, uh…

ANNA Don't think! First thing.

PATRICK Any night… with you.

Beat.

Want another sangria?

ANNA Uh…

PATRICK That's a yes.

ANNA No.

But he's already gone. Shift.

SCENE TWENTY-ONE

ANNA *hums "Sweet Dreams."*

STRANGER What are you singing?

Beat. He softly sings along with her…

SCENE TWENTY-TWO

PATRICK *comes back; they're now on top of a lookout.*

ANNA You're right, this *is* an amazing view.

PATRICK You never been up here?

ANNA Mn. Maybe in my teens. Came and parked.

PATRICK You and Ben?

ANNA I have had other boyfriends, you know.

PATRICK Really? You'd never know.

Hey, do you wonder if he still follows you sometimes?

ANNA He's just hurt.

PATRICK …'Kay, look. You see that tower with the big red lights?

ANNA Yeah.

PATRICK 'Kay, just below that, and a little to the left, you see that blue, kind of glowing—?

ANNA Oh, yeah, yeah…

PATRICK 'Kay, just above that… that little strip of lights there?

ANNA Yeah.

PATRICK The second one is our house.

ANNA Really?

PATRICK Yuh.

ANNA How can you tell?

PATRICK Come up here in the day, you can follow the roads, go by landmarks, anywhere you want.

ANNA Got a lot of time on your hands?

PATRICK Used to come up here a lot, yeah.

ANNA …So are you and Maddie related somehow?

PATRICK Mn, she's kind of like my second mom. Cuz when my parents died, she took me in.

…Oh. Yeah, my folks died when I was sixteen, and I ended up in the city, sort of staying in different places, on the street sometimes. Met Maddie at the shelter one night, cuz she volunteers there, and she decided to take me in. I'd take care of the house, and she'd give me room and board.

ANNA You were a street kid?

PATRICK Kind of, stayed in shelters or different people's places, yeah. But it's cool now, though. Now I volunteer at the shelters and some of the kitchens and stuff. And most of the web work I do is for places like that too. Feels nice to be able to give back now, you know?

ANNA Yeah…

Beat.

What happened to them?

PATRICK Oh, uh…. We lived on a farm and one night the house caught fire. The first thing to go was the roof, and my room was downstairs, so I got out, but… and I tried to, but I couldn't—get back in, you know.

ANNA You were sixteen?

He nods.

God, you seem so…

PATRICK Over it?

ANNA Whole.

PATRICK Well, time marches on, I guess.

ANNA My mom died just last year.

PATRICK God, I'm sorry. How?

ANNA Car accident.

PATRICK Where's your dad?

ANNA Remarried a long time ago.

PATRICK I guess we're both orphans then.

ANNA ...What do you think happens when you die?

PATRICK Depends. If you were good, maybe it's like a dream, you know? You meet up with someone you cared about in life, like their spirit or whatever. You go for a drive, nice dinner, maybe some lip-synch...

Beat.

ANNA And if you were bad?

PATRICK Well, then it's a nightmare.

ANNA ...How long did it take for you to just... let them go?

PATRICK Who says I have?

...Well, this is fun.

She smiles. They look out over the city.

ANNA — Out of all those lights. I had to pick that one.

I bet if we had a telescope we could see Colette's "Psychic" sign.

PATRICK — Oh God. "Vun of you vill die!"

ANNA — "And vun of you vill die inside!"

PATRICK — "Patsrick, zose seegarettes vill kill you!"

They laugh.

SCENE TWENTY-THREE

They're now back in ANNA's apartment.

PATRICK — Fun night.

ANNA — Yeah. Thank you.

PATRICK — Thank *you.*

A moment.

'Kay, I should let you go to sleep.

She nods.

I mean, it's not like there's not.... But we should.... I mean, you just moved in. It could get complicated.

And you just broke up. It would be messy.

And I don't wanna be… you know. Like a rebound. Or take advantage, or whatever.

Okay. I should…

Good night.

He leans in to definitely only kiss her cheek. She… allows it.

He turns to go, then stops.

Um.

He goes. She pulls him back and they kiss, hard, passionate. But then she pulls away.

ANNA *(smiles)* How do you know me so well?

He takes her face in both his hands and kisses her again, slowly.

They begin to make love.

SCENE TWENTY-FOUR

ANNA *lies in bed, alone.*

PATRICK *appears alone upstairs in his room, his headphones plugged into his laptop and watching the screen, the light from the images flickering on his face. And we hear what's coming through his headphones:*

PATRICK *(voice-over)* —and I don't wanna be… you know. Like a rebound. Or take advantage, or whatever.

(voice-over) Okay. I should…

(voice-over) Good night.

Sound of the kiss on the cheek.

(voice-over) Um.

Sound of kissing.

ANNA *(voice-over)* How do you know me so well?

PATRICK, *alone in his room, smiles…*

Music swells.

And we start to hear a bunch of different scenes from the play so far.

PATRICK Sleep well.

ANNA *sits up suddenly… and starts dancing raw and violent.*

The sound of a car crashing.

SCENE TWENTY-FIVE

PATRICK *enters* ANNA's *dance studio with two coffees.*

PATRICK Hey.

ANNA Oh, hey!

PATRICK Am I interrupting?

ANNA No, just rehearsing.

PATRICK Oh my God, look at this.

ANNA Yeah, this is my set. What are you doing here?

PATRICK Nothing, just in the area, thought I'd stop in, bring you a coffee.

ANNA I can't.

PATRICK It's decaf.

ANNA Aw…

PATRICK You busy, or…?

ANNA No, come in. I'll show you around.

PATRICK So how's it going? How's "Tortured" coming along?

ANNA Ugh. Don't know how to end it.

PATRICK Yeah, isn't that always the way?
What's it about?

ANNA Sleepwalking.

PATRICK Hm, you know anything about that?

ANNA …Confusional arousal.

PATRICK Mm, that sounds hot.

ANNA No, like the conscious and subconscious. The line between asleep and awake. I want the whole thing to feel like a maze.

PATRICK Well, good luck with that.

Aw, ballet bar.

ANNA Yup. And sprung floors. Soundproof walls. Aaagh! And we hung all the mirrors ourselves.

PATRICK Wow. This is awesome…

And I'm guessing bathrooms behind here?

ANNA And change rooms, yeah.

PATRICK 'Kay, gimme a sec.

He gives her a kiss, then leaves.

She puts down her coffee and practises a move in the mirror.

Shift.

SCENE TWENTY-SIX

She's now in the sleep lab. Voices over the speakers again:

PATRICK *(voice-over)* Here. They ran out of cream.

PETE *(voice-over)* Damn.

PATRICK *(voice-over)* How's our ballerina. Holy, she's still standing there?

PETE *(voice-over)* Yuh.

PATRICK *(voice-over)* She hasn't woken up?

PETE *(voice-over)* Nope.

On stage we see PATRICK in the bathroom of the studio, checking himself out in the mirror.

PATRICK *(voice-over)* Hey, what'll the doctors do for her, anyway?

PETE *(voice-over)* Oh, you know, psychotherapy, maybe hypnosis. And if nothing else works, they'll probably just give her drugs.

PATRICK *(voice-over)* You know what I'd do with a girl like that?

PETE *(voice-over)* What?

PATRICK *(voice-over)* Have her in every position imaginable, you know, non-stop.

PATRICK, in the bathroom, raises his shirt to reveal a hidden body camera taped to his chest. He turns it on.

PETE *(voice-over)* Patrick...

PATRICK *(voice-over)* I'm serious. I'm no doctor, but some good old-fashioned sex therapy. Only way a girl like that's gonna stop all that moving around, man. And relax, you know, just fuckin' *relax.*

PETE *(voice-over)* Well, thank God you're just the janitor.

PATRICK leaves the bathroom, returning to the studio.

PATRICK *(voice-over)* Yuh. I say it could all be solved with one good long continuous fuck.

PETE *(voice-over)* Jesus, Patrick. Shuffle the cards.

In the studio, PATRICK and ANNA stare at each other in the mirror. He kisses her lips, her neck, then makes his way down her body…

Shift.

SCENE TWENTY-SEVEN

ANNA's suddenly alone. A night terror.

ANNA I want out.

I want out!

ANNA grabs her keys, walks up the stairs. PATRICK sees her.

PATRICK Anna?

She leaves the house.

Anna?

She gets into her car and starts it.

Oh my God. Anna, you're in your car.

Anna, wake up, you're in your car!

She looks at him. He opens the door.

Sweetie… are you awake?

She bats out at him.

Anna—wake up!

She breathes out and awakes. Terrified.

SCENE TWENTY-EIGHT

They're now in her room. There are bars on the window.

PATRICK Are you sure about this?

ANNA Yes.

PATRICK Okay. Well, they lock and unlock, so you can still get out if you need to. Here's the key.

ANNA Where would I put it?

PATRICK Anywhere.

ANNA But then I can get to it. I can't keep the key in here.

Beat.

And I need to lock up my knives and things. Do you have padlocks?

PATRICK Yeah.

ANNA Good. I should put one on my door too.

PATRICK What? Anna no, you gotta be able to get out.

ANNA What do you want me to do? Go to sleep every night knowing I could wake up in head-on traffic?

PATRICK Well just lock up your car keys.

ANNA But what about the key?

PATRICK Jesus—use a combination!

ANNA I'll know it.

PATRICK In your sleep? Sweetie, I really think you're going too far.

ANNA I'm making it out to my car! What would have happened if you hadn't caught me? What would have happened?

PATRICK Then give me your car keys. Give them to *me*.

ANNA What?

PATRICK Simple. Done. Then you can't go anywhere.

ANNA I could still get out, into the street.

PATRICK I'm not locking you in here.

ANNA Fine, I'll do it myself. I'll lock myself in. And every night I'll slip the key under my door, and every morning you slip it back.

PATRICK Sweetie, maybe you should just go back to your doctor. Spend another night in that lab.

ANNA It's a three-month wait. What do I do in the meantime? Pray?

PATRICK Fine, then what if I stayed?

ANNA What?

PATRICK If you just let me stay with you for once. Watch over you.

ANNA You can't stay.

PATRICK What, I'm just supposed to fuck you and go back upstairs?

ANNA You can't stay! You don't understand. I don't know what I'll do.

PATRICK I'll protect you.

ANNA It's not about you. When I was little, I'd wake up with steak knives in my hands. When I was with Ben, there were times I woke up choking him.

PATRICK Well, I'm not Ben.

ANNA Listen to me! This is hereditary. My mom used to sleepwalk.

PATRICK So?

ANNA So one night she got up, walked out to her car—

Beat.

PATRICK Oh my God.

All right. I'll install a lock on the inside of your door.

ANNA Thank you.

PATRICK Another on a drawer where you can lock up your keys and anything sharp.

ANNA Thanks.

PATRICK And every night you can slip the key under, so you can't get at it. And every morning, I'll slip it back, so you can get out.

ANNA You're a lifesaver, thanks.

I do love you, you know.

PATRICK I know.

The sound of a lock closing.

Shift.

SCENE TWENTY-NINE

An alarm clock buzzes. It's the middle of the night. ANNA rolls over and turns it off.

She looks up at the ceiling.

PATRICK is above her in his room, typing on his computer.

ANNA reaches up, higher and higher…

PATRICK leans into his computer screen.

ANNA Patrick…?

PATRICK looks down to the vent, then back at his computer.

Patrick…

ANNA pulls down a tiny spy camera from out of the vent. It hangs by a wire.

You dropped something.

PATRICK *(mouthing)* Fuck!

ANNA stares at the camera. PATRICK doesn't know what to do.

ANNA breathes out on the camera lens. She's still asleep.

SCENE THIRTY

A flame is lit. PATRICK is holding it.

The fire alarm goes off. ANNA wakes with a jolt.

PATRICK Anna, wake up!

There's a fire! Get out! The key is under your door!

Jesus Christ—

ANNA opens her door.

It's a furnace fire, it's small, but okay; just go out back. *(into his phone)* Yeah, I need to report a small fire, 4950 Knight Street—

Anna, get outside! Go wake Maddie, I'll be out in a sec.

ANNA Are you okay?

PATRICK I got it, okay, just get out!

She goes.

Yeah, 4950 Knight Street, off Thirty-third…

ANNA's gone. PATRICK, alone now, hurries into her room. He gets up on her bed, clears the smoke, and unscrews the vent, where the camera still dangles.

SCENE THIRTY-ONE

ANNA's outside with MADDIE. While putting the camera back and screwing in the vent, PATRICK plays MADDIE's voice:

ANNA Maddie, you all right?

MADDIE I'm fine, I'm fine. Where is Patrick?

ANNA Still inside. Says it's something to do with the furnace, but he's got it under control.

MADDIE Let's pray that's true.

Beat.

ANNA This must be really hard on him.

MADDIE How's that?

ANNA Because of his parents.

MADDIE What?

ANNA Because of his parents.

MADDIE Hm?

ANNA Because of how his parents died.

MADDIE ...His parents died?

ANNA ...When he was sixteen...

MADDIE What?

ANNA When he was sixteen... in a fire.

MADDIE What are you talking about? I thought they lived just outside of town.

Beat.

ANNA Maddie, stay here, I'll be right back.

Patrick!

Patrick!

She runs…

SCENE THIRTY-TWO

ANNA's *now back inside; PATRICK is holding the camera.*

ANNA Patrick—

PATRICK Ah, Jesus—I thought I told you to stay outside!

ANNA What is that?

PATRICK Nothing, just a uh… snake camera. Using it to make sure nothing's blocking the vent. I'm a geek, I know; if they make it, I gotta have it. Get outta here, okay? I'll be out in a sec. Tell Maddie the fire truck's on its way.

Shift.

SCENE THIRTY-THREE

ANNA's *breath is quick and laboured.*

ANNA They're on their way?

STRANGER That's right, they're on their way. I'm looking after you.

ANNA You're looking after me?

STRANGER That's right.

ANNA You're watching me?

STRANGER That's right.

ANNA You're watching? You have a camera?

STRANGER Sorry?

ANNA A camera. A snake.

STRANGER Excuse me?

ANNA A snake.

Patrick!

Patrick!

She runs.

SCENE THIRTY-FOUR

ANNA bursts into PATRICK's room; he's at his desk.

PATRICK Oh, God… Jesus, what the hell?

She stares at his computer.

What? Oh man, yeah, crashes sometimes. Usually to do with magnetic fields… maybe it sensed your "magnetism"?

The joke is lost on her.

Don't worry, it's saved, just this… site I'm creating. So what the hell, don't you knock?

ANNA Sorry, my place is still smoky—can I come in?

PATRICK Uh, sure.

ANNA You got smoke in here too, huh?

PATRICK Yeah…

She goes to look at the vent under his desk.

What?

ANNA Nothing, nothing. Sorry, I'm a little out of it.

That must have been hard for you today, huh?

PATRICK What's that?

ANNA The fire…

PATRICK No, not really, I was lucky; got to it soon as it started.

ANNA No, I mean… having to go through it like that.

PATRICK Oh yeah. Yeah…

ANNA Is Maddie going senile?

PATRICK — What do you mean?

ANNA — I mean, is she losing it a bit?

PATRICK — Why?

I don't think so. Why?

ANNA — And was it a *girl* who lived here before?

PATRICK — Hm?

ANNA — A girl. Before me. Living down there.

PATRICK — Uh, yeah. Why?

ANNA — What was her name?

PATRICK — Uh, Rachel.

ANNA — Rachel— *(She shivers.)* I'm cold. And you said she was crazy?

PATRICK — I don't know…

ANNA — No, you said she was crazy.

PATRICK — Okay. What does it matter? Why do you care about the person before?

ANNA — I'm cold. I need to borrow something.

She opens his drawers.

PATRICK — Anna… what the hell? That's my stuff.

She pulls out wires, old computer parts.

Can you get outta there, please?

She pulls out a hospital uniform with a name tag.

Anna, give that here.

He reaches for it, but she keeps it.

This is my stuff. What's wrong with you?

She stares at the name tag.

Are you okay?

ANNA You work at the hospital?

He takes the scrubs.

PATRICK I volunteer there sometimes.

She looks back at the computer, the vent.

Sweetie, please, you're shaking.

He reaches out, but she bats him away. She backs out of the room.

What the hell—? Anna, what's wrong? Anna, talk to me. Anna, wait! What's wrong with you?!

Shift.

SCENE THIRTY-FIVE

Back to the sleep lab. ANNA's there.

And PATRICK's now in the sleep lab with her. He's wearing the uniform and name tag. ANNA is sleepwalking, having a nightmare, scared. PETE is still in voice-over:

PETE *(voice-over)* Patrick!

PATRICK Pete! Fuck, you scared me…

PETE *(voice-over)* What the hell? What are you doing?

PATRICK There's an intercom?

PETE *(voice-over)* Of course. What is this? I fall asleep for two minutes and this is what you do?

PATRICK Oh, don't be such a saint. She doesn't even know I'm in here, man!

PETE *(voice-over)* Of course not. Now get outta there, you wanna get me fired?

PATRICK snaps his fingers in ANNA's face and she reacts.

(voice-over) Patrick… I'd watch it if I were you, they can get violent.

PATRICK Really?

PETE *(voice-over)* Yeah, you never heard of Ken Parks? Killed his mother-in-law in his sleep.

PATRICK Holy shit.

PETE *(voice-over)* Yeah, stabbed her to death. So quit horsing around.

PATRICK Has she been violent?

PETE *(voice-over)* I don't know.

PATRICK Yes you do— Is this her file?

PETE *(voice-over)* Hey. Get out of that. Come on now, out.

PATRICK *(reading her file)* Man, it's all in here…

PETE *(voice-over)* That's it, I'm coming in there.

PATRICK Violent nightmares. Choreographer.

PETE *(voice-over)* Patrick, you better have your ass out by the time I get there.

PATRICK Mother deceased. Engaged. Shit, you're engaged?

PATRICK *reaches for* ANNA's *hand; she lashes out—*

ANNA I want out!

PATRICK Whoa! *(laughs)* Okay. What?

ANNA Ben, I want out.

PATRICK Ben? Okay. You do? Out of what?

ANNA I need to be alone.

I need to find my own place.

PATRICK Yeah? Where you gonna go?

ANNA I don't know. But I'm looking for my own place.

PATRICK ...I'll find you one. I know a great basement suite.

He touches her face.

You're stunning.

PETE *(voice-over)* You're on tape, asshole!

PATRICK Oh shit!

PATRICK goes to leave.

Hey Pete, you can cut that out, right?
Shuffle 'em up, your deal.

(to ANNA*)* Good night!

PATRICK fades out of view. ANNA turns down to the mirror.

SCENE THIRTY-SIX

Knock, knock, knock.

PATRICK It's Patrick.

The light from her sliver-moon mirror rises. She's now in her room.

ANNA Come in.

He does.

PATRICK Hey. You wanted the drill…?

ANNA Great, thanks.

PATRICK You doing okay?

ANNA Yeah, sorry about taking off like that. I hadn't eaten anything all day, the fire freaked me out. I was totally out of it.

PATRICK You're telling me.

ANNA I can be a bit of a wackjob.

PATRICK Was there something…? I mean, I volunteer at a hospital sometimes, is that… weird for some reason?

ANNA No. Just the same hospital where I slept in that lab.

PATRICK Oh.

ANNA Anyway, sorry if I scared you, I think I just needed some air.

PATRICK Where'd you go?

ANNA Just for a drive.

She starts unscrewing the bars from her window.

PATRICK What are you doing?

ANNA	Taking these down.
PATRICK	Why?
ANNA	Don't think I need 'em. Took down all the locks too.
PATRICK	What?
ANNA	Yeah, it really feels better.
PATRICK	What the hell? What's going on?
ANNA	Turning over a new leaf.
PATRICK	What do you mean—are you… moving out?
ANNA	No.
PATRICK	And you're sleeping here tonight?
ANNA	Yeah.
PATRICK	Sorry, Anna, what's going on?
ANNA	Nothing, I just don't want to live like this anymore.
PATRICK	Like what?
ANNA	Caging myself in—bars, locks, pills—I can't.
PATRICK	Wait, you're still taking your Diazepam though, right?
ANNA	Nope, flushed it.
PATRICK	What?!

ANNA Well, not the bottle, just the pills. The bottle I threw in the garbage.

The bars are now off her window.

I'm gonna put these out here.

She does. PATRICK scans the room. ANNA comes back.

PATRICK Sorry, Anna, what's going on?!

ANNA Are your parents alive?

PATRICK What?!

ANNA Are they alive?

PATRICK What? No. What? What is this?

ANNA Maddie told me they live just outside of town.

PATRICK She what? Well, she's obviously confused, she's eighty-two years old.

And you believe her?

ANNA Why would she lie?

PATRICK Why would I?

ANNA I don't know.

Beat.

PATRICK You want me to go ask her?

Fine, I'll go ask her right now. I'll bring her right down.

He goes to leave, but turns back.

You know what, this is fucked. You're— I love you and you're—

Her phone rings. She goes to answer.

Anna. Anna, what the fuck?

ANNA Hello?

Ben, yeah.

Twenty minutes?

'Kay, see ya then.

She hangs up.

PATRICK You're going to see him?

ANNA Yeah.

PATRICK This is a guy that was stalking you.

ANNA Patrick—

PATRICK This is a guy that was checking your email, following you, didn't you say?

ANNA I thought, maybe.

PATRICK So you're gonna see him again.

ANNA Yes.

PATRICK And you think that's a good idea.

ANNA Yes.

PATRICK ...Sorry, sweetie, I just want you to be safe.

ANNA I will be.

Oh.. Here. Don't need these anymore.

She hands the padlocks back.

Good night.

He doesn't move.

Good night.

PATRICK Good night.

Shift.

SCENE THIRTY-SEVEN

PATRICK *is up in his room, on his computer.*

ANNA *sleeps.*

After a moment, she sits up. She has a butcher knife in her hand.

PATRICK *leans into his screen.*

ANNA gets up, wanders a bit, staring at the blade.

She makes her way up the stairs.

PATRICK looks over his shoulder.

ANNA stops. She goes back down into her room. She is stopped by her reflection in the mirror.

PATRICK looks back at his computer.

ANNA, staring at herself, breathes out on the glass.

She breathes out again, more urgently.

She raises the knife to herself.

PATRICK Anna—!

PATRICK bolts out of his room.

SCENE THIRTY-EIGHT

PATRICK is at ANNA's door.

PATRICK Anna…!

Anna, wake up! You've got a knife.

He comes in.

Sweetheart, wake up, you're holding a knife…

ANNA I know…

PATRICK What?

ANNA I know.

Suddenly the knife's at his throat and he's down on the ground.

PATRICK What do you mean? What are you doing?

ANNA Where is it?

PATRICK What?

ANNA The camera. Where is it?

PATRICK Camera? What? Are you awake?

ANNA I've been awake all night. Lying there, pretending to sleep. Listening to you listening to me. Listening to you watching me.

PATRICK Watching you? What?

ANNA I could hear you get scared when I pulled this out. Your little footsteps, the creaking floor.

PATRICK What are you…? No, I was— I couldn't sleep, I went out for a walk, and when I came back I saw in your window—

ANNA I could hear you upstairs.

PATRICK But I swear, I just saw in your window—

ANNA I could hear you upstairs!

PATRICK It was in your mind!

ANNA No— I've lost a lot of things, but as much as you might wish, I have not lost my fucking mind. Yet. But I'm about to if I don't get some answers—now where is it?

Where is it?

PATRICK Ow, ow—okay, okay. Just calm down, okay? Seriously, just listen to me. I don't know what kind of nightmares you've been having tonight, but—

ANNA *(tightening the blade to his throat)* No, you listen to me—this is *your* nightmare—I can do anything I want right now. You realize that? This could look like sleepwalking, self-defence, anything. And I'd totally get away with it. You do not know how close I am to the edge, all right? I don't know if *you* broke my window when I first moved in—

PATRICK What?

ANNA If you drugged me that night so you could hide a camera—

PATRICK Drugged you? How?

ANNA —but I do know a couple things: one, I am so awake right now, you wouldn't believe it; two, there is a camera in this room, my conscious, my subconscious, all my fucking consciousnesses are screaming it out to me; and three, if they're not calmed down, they're going to explode. So I'll make it easy. You're just going to answer "yes" or "no." Is it in the vent there? Yes or no.

PATRICK No, Anna.

ANNA The light switch.

PATRICK No—

ANNA The plug-in, the corner—

PATRICK No— I don't even know what you're talking about!

ANNA Then why aren't you screaming, huh? If you don't know what I'm talking about, why don't you scream and wake everyone up?

Your door is open, isn't it?

And we're on there right now.

Aren't we?

Aren't we?

All right. Why don't we go have a look?

She turns to go.

PATRICK Okay, wait. Okay, okay, just… *(She swipes at him.)* Ah, fuck. Okay, just wait. It's not what you think. It's not what you think, I swear— I just put it in tonight.

I swear. I just put it in. I was so worried— You had me so worried! You weren't taking your pills, you took off your locks— I love you— I love you, and I'm sitting there watching you about to stab yourself in your sleep—can you imagine what that did to me?

ANNA I wanna see where it is.

PATRICK Anna—

She swipes at him.

Fuck, fuck, okay, okay.

He points to the vent.

I just put it in tonight, I swear.

ANNA When?

PATRICK When you went out with Ben. I was so worried.

ANNA How'd you get in?

PATRICK My key.

ANNA Your key.

He nods.

I changed my locks.

Beat.

PATRICK Oh. Yeah. I know.

ANNA You know.

PATRICK Yeah.

ANNA How?

PATRICK I uh… tried to get in during the fire. Realized the locks were changed.

ANNA So you made a copy?

PATRICK Yeah.

ANNA Today.

PATRICK Yeah.

ANNA With what key? With the key I had with me all day?

She swipes at him.

PATRICK Jesus Christ, can you put that down, please?

What did you think? That I'd watched you before?

You know what I think? I think Ben destroyed you. I think he destroyed your ability to trust anymore. So things are good but you get scared. You start having anxiety, nightmares you can't explain. Cuz there is no explanation except you got some deep-seated fear you gotta get over.

I mean, what on earth possessed you to do that tonight? I can't believe you would do that. You really think I'm that sick? How do you think that makes me feel?

ANNA And what if I can't believe you?

PATRICK What?

ANNA What if I can't believe you? What if I don't?

PATRICK Anna…

ANNA How do I *know* I can trust you, Patrick? How do I *know*?

PATRICK You don't.

That's what trust is.

Beat.

The alarm clock goes off.

He shuts it off.

Beat.

ANNA Holy fuck.

PATRICK What?

ANNA Open it.

She thrusts the alarm clock into his hands.

Open it!

Confused, PATRICK looks at it, then at her. He smiles, then holds the alarm clock up to her.

PATRICK Smile.

He shoves it in her face and forces her onto the bed. Pinning her down and choking her.

You crazy fucking bitch!

If you just believed me, you'd be totally fine. We'd be in love, you'd be happy. But it's the fucking fear that gets in the way, you know that? Rachel was exactly the same.

Although she was less exciting. Not enough entertainment for the twenty-four-hour viewers. Even the sex was boring. But you… all the shit you do in your sleep? Man, from the moment I saw you asleep in that lab, I knew you'd be a fucking gold mine. Do you know how much money you made me? World Without Borders? Ha. Try House Without Borders.

But don't worry, it's not live. I'll edit this before I upload. Show you in your best light. My guys aren't into snuff.

ANNA I loved you. I totally loved you. More than I ever have.

PATRICK I know.

He goes to grab the knife—

She breathes out on his face.

He stops. Is she asleep?

She slices his gut. He falls.

She tries to run.

But he grabs her, pulls her back, and their bodies collide.

Beat.

He backs away. Stabbed.

He falls.

She looks at the knife in her hands. Drops it.

He sinks, dying.

ANNA Patrick…?

Patrick!

Patrick…

She panics.

She grabs her keys… and runs outside.

SCENE THIRTY-NINE

Sound of a speeding car.

The STRANGER appears.

A car crashes. Breaking glass. Fire.

The STRANGER cradles ANNA in his arms…

STRANGER Okay, stay with me.

ANNA One of us will die, and one of us will die inside.

STRANGER It'll be all right.

ANNA But I can't tell which.

STRANGER I'm right here, trust me. No one will die.

ANNA Patrick…

STRANGER Just trust me.

ANNA Patrick.

STRANGER Who?

ANNA Patrick!

STRANGER I'm not Patrick.

Beat.

ANNA I think I just killed someone.

STRANGER I doubt that.

ANNA I'm cold.

STRANGER I know.

ANNA I'm thirsty.

STRANGER I know, just stay with me.

ANNA I'm suffocating.

STRANGER Shh, you're gonna be okay. The ambulance is on it's way.

ANNA They're on their way?

STRANGER That's right, they're on their way. I'm looking after you.

ANNA You're looking after me?

STRANGER That's right.

ANNA You're watching me?

STRANGER That's right.

ANNA Where am I?

STRANGER On the side of the road.

ANNA There's stars on the ground…

STRANGER It's glass.

ANNA There's glass everywhere…

STRANGER You were in an accident. You hit a pole.

ANNA Where's my car?

STRANGER Over there. It's on fire.

Beat.

ANNA I just got tired.

Tired of ever letting down another wall.

But 'cause life with walls is no life at all

I closed my eyes.

Beat.

What's your name?

STRANGER Robert.

ANNA You have a very kind face, Robert.

Beat. She begins to gasp for air.

ROBERT What are you doing? Stay with me. What are you doing? Stay with me.… Stay with me…

She breathes out.

The end.

MICHAEL RUBENFELD

Michael Rubenfeld is the artistic producer of the SummerWorks Theatre Festival (circa 2008). He is also an independent theatre artist. His work includes: *The Book of Judith* (co-created with Sarah Stanley), *My Fellow Creatures, Spain* (SummerWorks 2004) and *Present Tense* (SummerWorks 2003). He has also directed *Essay* by Hannah Moscovitch (SummerWorks 2005) and *Yogyakarta* by Alan Dilworth (SummerWorks 2007). Michael is a graduate of the National Theatre School.